Greater Than

Life's Journey Through Poetry

Writings By:

Halima A. Brown

Contents

Dedication

For My Heavenly Father, My God, My Daddy, My Lord. God you are the one who has loved me back to life. Your love for me continues to call me closer to you daily. Thank you, Lord, for telling me that I can do *Greater Than*. Here I am Lord. Here we are. I love you Lord.

For Every Woman, you are strong, pull from your inner strength. You are loved, know always that God loves you. To all my Sisters and Sisters in Christ, we.

For You the Reader. Thank you for unknowingly inspiring me to share this work with you. I encourage you to live, to love, to learn, and search your heart. Have a journey worth exploring and enjoying for the rest of your lifetime. Write your own story it's worth sharing and being heard.

Acknowledgements

Thank you to my sisters **Shamelle, Anita, Shannel and Asha**. Ladies your love for me is inspiring. To my sister Anita, your poetry as a youth inspired me beyond words, your faith, and intellect gives me life. Thank you for sharing your talent with me, it is still such a blessing. To all my **Sisters in Christ** that are all over the world, your good sister love hits my heart., by the thought of you.

Special thank you to **Rachelle Curry** for helping me move from scared and homeless, to brave and alive. Rachelle, I love you. **Sacouya Chandler**, for helping me change my life. You don't know what you did for me that night we moved mattresses on our heads. Thank you and know that I love you. Special thanks to my brothers Nicholas, Shamari and Mwata for supporting me during this healing process.

Thank you to all my wonderful **Teachers and Professors**. You all pushed me to be more, and always believed that I would be able to do everything I set out to do in life. With the absence of parents in my life, you were all great helps raising me. You all didn't know it then, but you all helped save my life as I clung to school as a safe place and an escape during childhood.

Lastly to Life for always giving me something to write about.

Introduction

Greater Than is a letter to the Lord; that I have held inside my heart for years. It's not always a sweet love letter, and most of the time it's ugly, and too honest for my eyes to bare at times. This book of poetry is like my heart. With lines from me to God. I was broken into pieces and I almost died to write this book. And as I wrote more and more, I began to realize that as much as I almost died to write this book, I have also lived for this very moment as well.

Greater Than: Life's Journey Through Poetry is the brain child of a nervous breakdown. I had several life events that landed me in the hospital. I didn't understand it then, but I needed to break, not spiritually, but emotionally and mentally. All the pain I held inside of me, was the same pain that was killing me. This nervous breakdown was a cry to the world, to my family, and to myself that I needed help. I needed to know that I was not okay. The early success I had in my life, was not a reflection of a healthy mental state. Instead showed my ability to function in the pain, depression, and anxiety.

At the time of the nervous breakdown, no one in my family knew that I had been molested and raped for years. No one knew, that I had been forced to live a double life. The nervous breakdown changed that. I was twenty-five when I vocalized the sexual abuse that I had endured for years. Suddenly the secret was out.

I remember explaining what happened to me, to my younger siblings in Canada, they felt horrible for me. I felt horrible for them feeling horrible, but I told them I was okay. I was. I explained to them, that I didn't mean to lie, they explained to me, that I didn't need to feel bad for lying, we cried, and hugged, and cried and hugged some more. That was not an easy process. I see now how free I am at this very moment. Yet, even more important than sharing that part of my life; is the fact that I have learned to live. I've learned to love despite the adversities in my life.

After sharing what happened to me with a few family members a select number of friends, I stopped living a life filled with lies. I didn't have to protect myself, God was doing it for me. The secret of what happened to me wasn't protecting me, it was hurting me. Letting it go was a new good, and a different new that I had to slowly learn to love and appreciate. I'm continuously learning how to function in this new life, and the new freedoms are great.

Writing Great Than: Life's Journey Through Poetry was one of my greatest artistic challenges to date. As I struggled through seemingly endless pages of scribbled emotions, my eyes welled with water. I sifted through poems, wrote and rewrote poems. I grew new arteries in my chest, that linked to parts of my heart that I never knew existed as I completed certain poems. Arteries leading to parts of my that once kept me from breathing correctly. Now, I can breathe. This completed work is my love offering to the Lord God, to Myself, and to you the Reader. I hope that this serves you fully.

What is this about? Greater Than: Life's Journey Through Poetry, is a decree of deliverance and freedom through poetic expression. It is an announcement that the silence that surrounds sexual abuse in children and adult is broken. A decree that God's people: children and adults are free from the hands of their enemies. That God's children are free from abuse, and free from those who abuse their authority and power. A decree that the children of God are safe, are protected, are love, and are not forgotten. That they should no longer fear, instead believe and trust in the powerful love that is God. Survivors of abuse are no longer controlled by anxiety, depression, lack, loss, and hopelessness, but instead God's children are free from anxiety, depression, loss and lack. This story depicts some of the work it will take to live and thrive in this new place of hope and love. I think that we as God's children and God's people have to give ourselves permission to let go of the past pain and wrongdoings. It takes work, but you deserve the work it takes to have the life you want. I am living witness that it's possible to be free, to love, to learn, to grow, and have a life that is worthy of the GREATNESS that is on the inside us.

I encourage all those reading who need support to seek help from safe places. Safe places, with individuals that value you, care for you, and want the best for you. If you can go to therapy (individual or group therapy), self-help groups, church groups, and so many others. Go for you! You can also start your own support group. Whatever you do, keep giving yourself opportunities to live and have your best life. I hope you can get to a place of self-love, and gain new perspectives in your life. Love yourself you deserve it. You deserve the best you. In life love is going to be the force, the energy, the power that changes you. A pure kind and patient Love.

Now as young-women I use poetry to gaze back into my childhood and adolescences to bring you "Greater Than: Life's Journey Through Poetry." This was a 6 ½ year personal writing journey to compile this work. I invite you, to take the journey with me. So, get a glass of your favorite drink or listen to your favorite music as you read this story from hurt, heartbreaks, to healing, peace, love, and joy. I use the art of poetry to willing open the ugliest and most heart-aching parts of my life. If one other person can be helped my story, my entire life is worth living. For those who share in this pain, or a similar pain, be strong, you are coming out of it, you will survive, you have more life to live. Thank you for not giving up on you, thank you for continuing to fight for your life. To anyone who have never endured a similar life, I am blessed to know you don't have to relate personally to understand, so I thank you for you. We are Survivors! We are alive! We have survived!

Be your own GREATER THAN.

Chapter One

Past Pain

The Greatest Depression

Part One

The truth shall set you free.
But how can you be set free by the truth, if you don't know the truth?
How can I be who I am supposed to be — if I don't know who She is?
Or if I am able be her?

What and who do I have to look to?

How can I lift myself up, by myself?
How can I learn to grow up, when I never had a suitable atmosphere?
With an early environment of neglect, brutality, evil, and sexual abuse.
What am I supposed to do with that?

What do I truly have to look forward to?

Showers

Wash me with your living water.
Just like you did on Calvary.
Cleanse me with your blood.
Let my life be cleansed by your love.

Your obedience.
Your sacrifice.

You've done so much for me.
I want to think of nothing but your love for me.
I want to only remember your sacrifice for me.
Let that shower me daily.

Oh, Lord.
The shower, it's where the offense happened.

Oh, Lord, the shower is where one man decided that he was God.
One evil thought, that attempted to create a new existence for me life.
That shower washed me with death and lies.
Oh, my Lord the devil has had me in a choke hold, in the shower.

For years, I have feared being alone.
Then when it's time to shower, I cower.

 I remember the night the rapist crept into my bedroom.
After I accidently walked in that bathroom—curtains closed, and my head was down.
My head was down and all I was saw his blur behind shower curtains—I walked out.
I didn't see him naked, but to him I did, that beginning of molested, then raped.

I was raped due to fictitious lies.
Evil lies, evil man, devil with a plan to use an evil mind, and I was a child.

Lord, I remember he told me, 'I saw him naked in the shower,
so said he had to see me naked too.'
Why would he say that, 'God told him to do it? Why, so many lies?
Lord, remember when I wondered why?

Why? Why was I molested, why was I raped?
Why? Why me? Why was this why killing me?

Why did my father give me over to someone he barely knew?
Why did it have to be me?
Why didn't I take off running after school?
Where would I run to?

Where?
Where?

So, now showers scare me.
Showers make me cry.
Showers sometimes make me want to die.
But I need to take showers.

Showers make you clean, they purify you.
I need to shower. I need to function in life.

Still those showers aren't the washing of your blood.
Still these showers aren't like when you rose up and left that tomb.
When I'm alone in the tub. I feel so afraid. I cannot do this without you.
Lord your life was all I needed then, and is all I need now.

Lord shower me. Lord shower with me. Purify me.
Lord Shower me. Rain on me. Reign on the inside of me, and reign over me.

Lord, so that I can shower again.
So, I can see you clearly, without the distorted vision I was cursed with years ago.
Lord wash the pain away, wash the abuse away, wash the curse away in the shower.
Make it so I can shower again, without thinking about years of agony.

Lord, shower me with your love.
Lord, shower me with your love.

Lord, you've done so much for me.
I want to think of nothing but your love for me.
I want to remember your sacrifice for me.
And let that shower me daily.

Your obedience.
Your sacrifice. Let that shower me.

Wash me with your living water.
Just like you did on Calvary.
Cleanse me with your blood.
And let my life be cleansed by your love.

Raped Me

Innocence was ripped from my chest,
gouged from my underwear,
as my childhood was crippled by the hands of my enemy.
A weak black African-American man defiled my innocence.
As the rapist arranged his large body beside my teenage body—to break and hold me,
he told me if I tell anyone he'd kill me.
He raped me, night after night when he taught to, and for 6 years I was a sex slave.
The devil must have rejoiced, while God must have wept.

I wanted to keep fighting, to keep fighting for my life.
But my fight turned into a freeze, and my legs couldn't free me—I was frozen.
AND I STOPPED kicking and screaming, and he assaulted me and took the virginity of a 14-year-old girl.
How could I keep fighting while my body was trapped under his heavy naked sweating body?
Raping me, kissing me like I was a woman, when I was a child.
I cried, and cried, I hated him.
But then I hated me, he raped me, and I....
I hated me for being raped.

I froze, I didn't run—I stayed.
I stayed, and I hated myself for not saving myself.
I'd belittle me, to preserve me.
Day after day telling myself how stupid I must be to be raped almost daily.
Years and years of self-loathing damaged my mind,
my soul, and my body years after.
How stupid I must be to not run away while everyone was sleeping?
But where would I go in a country I don't know?

That wicked man convinced himself that raping a 14-year-old was right.
Talk about evil intent.
Another rapist that is walking around free in the streets of New York.
For others it could have been another child, or a woman who raped them, but for he was a black man—damn.
The devil must have rejoiced at the thought that he had taken my faith.
What a plan the devil must had thought up— "another girl as a sex slave."
It made me broken, and weak, my soul was deteriorating inside of me.
It made not know my worth, so I hated myself instead of helping myself—I was young.

And now this guy stands in front of me,

telling me, there's not enough black women appreciating black men.

Looking back at him, I could only find his ignorance grossly unattractive.

Telling me I'm a trader to my kind.

As if being with a black man makes me black.

What the hell is my kind—Is "Black Love" the only kind of love I can have?

Black Love jargon and Ignorant men don't mix.

Some men have no clue what they are saying—or better yet who they are talking to.

Men who want date, but don't know how to talk to a woman.

Foolish men telling me I hate them, because is don't want them.

Men don't keep letting the devil use you, fool you, trap you, and kill you.

Don't live off his lies. The Devil is a lair.

We should know men, women of all races violate and rape—this is an ugly fact to face.

Men, women, raping, molesting, abusing vulnerable children.

Childhood stolen, violated, as they silently die for another man's sins.

Don't we see this is killing our communities.

Raped—it seized me for years.

But I am going to get my life back.

It took years for me to run away, but I got brave one day.

I ran away, I ran away from that rapist.

I ran away from the house of rape.

I ran away from rape.

Then I faced it alone, by myself, no one knew, until my life gave it away.

Today, I am no longer afraid of my thoughts of unworthiness and self-loathing,

Not hostage to what people might say.

I was raped for years, and I was molested as a child.

I lived through my own brokenness alone and in pain.

I am brave, yes I am bold, yes I am audacious, yes I am brilliant, yes I am free.

Now I live, love, and breath in life as I learn to live again.

I am Survivor, I am alive. We are Survivors. We have survived. We are alive.

Numbers

Seven, the first birthday I had without my Mother. I didn't know it then, but the next few years with my Mommie would be priceless. Mom, they were unforgettable. Thank you.

Eight, the no one loved me, but my older brother. A brother that fought for my life, every day of his.

Nine, the year I first wanted to die, I hated my home life.

Ten, fourth grade, the year I learned to dance the salsa, and the tango. Best year ever!

Eleven, the first time I could remember my father on earth celebrating my birthday with me. He threw me a birthday party! Also, the same year my father decided he could no longer raise my older brother and I.

Then he gave us up.

Twelve, the year my life would never be the same. The year I as first molested. First kiss on the lips, and way too much touching for two twelve-year-old. Was me having a boyfriend the reason I got?

Thirteen, I wanted to die. I remember hating my life. I attempted to kill myself almost daily. Summertime was fun away from the house. My friends were awesome, but knew nothing of the life I lived once in that house.

That dreadful house.

Fourteen, innocent, first time I was raped. Screaming "NO, NO, NO, NO, NO...," Hoping that the crack in the window was enough for the neighbors to hear my yells. It wasn't.

Fifteen, most of my friends had crushes or boyfriends. I lied to my friends, like I had a boyfriend too.

Sixteen, the year I wanted to run away. She confronted me and told me not to. The guardian that my father put me in care of. My sixteenth birthday, parents visited. I wanted to leave with my parents, but fear crippled me.

Seventeen, I was in love. I met this boy at a poetry slam, and it was love at first line. His parents hated me, because of the color of my skin. He was hated by the rapist that I lived with. We didn't last.

Eighteen, I went away. There's a place called Upward Bound, it saved my life. Every summer in high school I would go there, and one summer it in was Buffalo. Eighteen I ran away from that house, after I returned that summer. I wanted to be free. Free.

Nineteen, I met the wrong guy. I thought I was happy, and that I had what I wanted. Someone who loved me.

Twenty, hoping I don't get kicked out of college. Held hostage, by the man I thought loved me, missed midterm, because he tried to kill me. Finally, I left him.

Twenty-one, fell in love for the second time. We had a something good, I thought. We lost it. Aborted.

Twenty-three, I graduated with a social work degree.

Twenty-five, I had nervous breakdown. I guess I couldn't keep holding everything in.

Twenty-eight, I hear God say "Enough, enough." I had to stop living my life, my life running away from my past, and holding onto the pain of it all. I had to start fulling living God life for me.

Thirty, I decided I would love me, and learn from my mistakes. I needed change, so I moved across the country.

Numbers, you've haunted me for years, reminding me of the devils' plot to kill me.

Numbers, playing a revolving reel of abandonment, abuse, hate and hurt.

Numbers, I wish I could see straight, but at times numbers you blind me.

Numbers, I need you to turn back into just numbers again.

Puzzled Past

Tomorrow's regrets,
yesterday's fret after fret, after fret.
Today's heart pains leak blood from my chest to my feet.
Seductive words buckle my knees,
sending signals to my brain telling me this might be the one.
Slowly my feelings take over and my brain believes the stories told.
As my heart remembers love stories of old.
Should I stay, or should I go?

Love stories like roses with hidden thorns.
Kisses that blind-sided my better judgment.
Empty relationships, and a-could-be turned into a meant to be.
Where did I go wrong?
Hidden agenda wrapped up in pretty bows.
Laughter and tears. Hope mixed with fears.
What I called love was confusion draped up in bad relationships.
Lost in dead relationships, because of unresolved past problems.

When I was a kid.
Happy with friends but lying to them.
Great in school, playing the happy girl with no problem.
Everyone in school believed an outward act, called my sanity.
The fact I was dying inside. The puzzle pieces weren't fitting.
But what if others would have known?
Would I have been the raped girl, and how could she fit in?
No. I would have been the brave girl.

As an adult shame and sorrow try to linger in my todays,
and continuously try to haunt tomorrows.
My past is ugly.
It is dark.
My past is beautiful.
It is a flower closed.
It is a shadow.
This is my puzzled past.

Suicide

All I thought about was death.
Death and dying, and my blood on the floor.
Who would miss me.
What people would say?
Would I make my sisters mad?
Would they live a better life after I was gone?

I've habitually struggled in life.
Thinking about how my actions would merit death.
Thinking I was the judge to execute that punishment.
I've always wanted to live my life to the fullest.
I never had a role model, but I wish I could be a role model.
I want to be better for me and for you.

I used to think about dying daily.
killing myself,
and ending my life.
Now I see that my life has great value.
I have a life worth living—I want to live.
A life where I no longer want to end it all.

I no longer look at death as an option for myself.
I see suicide for what it is.
Suicide is a lie, that is lined with fear and doubt.
That fear is not from God, but from the devil.
It is a trick from the devil to take the lives of God's Chosen People.
God loves me, and God loves us.

God loves me, God loves you.
My life is treasured by God. Your life is treasured by God.
God has chosen me to live, God has chosen you to live.
We are chosen. We are Loved. Our life matters.
We are not a victim of the lies, that wants to tie you to death.
Love yourself, and love your life, and think—No more suicide."

The Greatest Depression

Part Two

How can I elevate myself when I'm down in a pit?
Can I help myself get up from this depression?
What have I learned, and what has my environment taught me?
What life skills can I use to lift myself out of this pit?
Is there something that I missed?

Does the environment need to be flawless, faultless to be suitable?
Should those in the environment need to invest their time in my life?
Tell me, is a perfect pretty neighborhood what will make the difference?
What does it take to make it? Will life make me or break me?
Will I rise above these depths of death to reach my something greater?

Setback, after setback, and inside my heart aches.
Painful thoughts and memories of things others have no idea about.
Memories, about my life that caused me to doubt, doubt—me.
The greatest depression is a mindset of perpetual defeat.
Lost in a pit of fear, and in need of strength.

I want to shout, I am tired of this.
Tired of wondering if the people who say they love me, love me.
I guess what life would be like without them in it?
Then I wonder if that life, and this life would be any different?
Does anyone care?

Why is it that no-one stands behind me?
In need of someone who is willing to help me stand.
A smile or a reaching hand, something to help me stand.
I'm asking but I get no answer.
When will God intervene?

What would I do to rid myself of the excruciating sensation of depression?
What is a good night's sleep, in a life filled with misery?
When can I rest assure?
When can I rest from the sorrow that keeps me down?
Who will intervene?

Does anyone care, and when will God intervene during this great depression?

Locked Up

I've never been a caged bird.
But I remember when I once sung beautiful songs.
I remember I would dance rhythmically through my day.

But—I was locked up,
and shut up,
and alone.

I feel the limbs of a once agile dancer, start to feel like a wilted dying plant.
I've never been a widow,
But feel as if my life has died and left me here alone to fend for myself.

I've never been a cat, but I've survived at least 5 out my 9 lives.
I've never been the wind, but I've been blown around, and around, and around, and
around, and around, and around again.

Let me out of this life.
Locked up in that prison life that should have never been.
Let me in, let me into the life that I know belongs to me.

I don't want this whirl wind to brutishly tosses me about any longer.
I don't want the wind to carry me away.
I don't want the sand to make me sink.

I want my feet to be planted on a strong foundation.
"I WANT IN."
I want in from this storm of life. Let me into the life that I know belongs to me.

Tearless

Last night I tried to cry.
I thought I would wash some of the sorrow out of my eyes.

My eyes ran dry, my tear ducts were all cried out.
I rubbed my waterless dry eyes, and I cried from the inside.

I know that the lack of tears
must mean even my body doesn't want me to hurt anymore.

So, I pulled my woman essence close to my chest.
Suddenly the hurt subsided from my breast and I felt at ease.

Thank God, I found some hope at the end of my tearless fit.
Some nights I feel no pain, sometimes not for months or weeks.

The pain I felt last night had been years old.
Today I hold onto the Holy Spirit, and now my spirit and woman are whole.

Unforgotten

Lord God Empty my heart.
Lord God Empty my mind.

As jagged edged memories pound against my brain.
I wonder how?
How did this memory get here?
How did it find its way to the front of my mind?

Hidden agendas,
and painful lies,
I thought I had forgotten,
all the agonizing pieces of my past.

Regrettably I had only shaded my present, with past painful memories.
With new memories not as painful, but those memories are deadly.
Those memories are silent,
they aggravate my present cognizance and try to kill my future.

Lord God please empty my heart.
Lord God Empty my mind.

Chapter 1 Breakdown

Chapter One: Past Pain

This chapter focuses on the hurt done to me during my child, early adolescence. There are some poems in this chapter that made me want to stop writing this poetry book. I remember thinking "I'm going too far, I'm saying too much." It took a great deal of strength to write this chapter. The immense amount of pain in my childhood was the catalyst to disconnect, and rupture within myself, and my family structure.

The Greatest Depression: Part One

This poem is about the struggle that someone has helping themselves up from a difficult life events without help from family or their community.

Showers

Shower was one of the most difficult poems I've ever written in my 20 years of writing poetry. This poem is about me accidently walked into the bathroom, because I heard what sound like me name being called. I totally was confused as to why, the man who was the boyfriend of my guardian be calling me, yet I went into the linen closet got the shampoo. A few days later, he told me that, because I saw him naked he would have to see me naked, so he came into the bathroom while I was in the shower and looked at me for a few minutes, then walked out. I was 12 years old.

Showers became difficult for years as an adult. To help myself, I would pray while taking showers and talk to YHWH/God in my mind, while rushing to get out of the shower.

Raped Me

I was 12 years old when I was raped at age 14, and then raped repeatedly until age 18.

This poem is my first time being open and saying I was raped in a poem, I've used so much code poetry lingo in the as a teenager, because it was still happening.

The second part of the poem is a commentary to black men; that I'm guessing down like to turned down by anyone.

Numbers

For some reason, I started to look at numbers in a bizarre way. If I thought of 12, I'd think of the year I was molested, if I thought of 18, I thought about the year, I ran away. Each number as I counted in my mind, would trigger a flashback to a painful memory.

Puzzled Past

This poem focuses on me being an adult and dating, and how confusing it was as an adult being of age to date, but being haunted by my childhood.

Suicide

There was a time, after I was being molested, and then raped that I use to try to kill myself about every day. I would get home from school, and try to cut my wrist almost every day, because I knew that night I would hear my door knob turn, and that meant I was going to be raped that night. It took, my leaving for one summer out of the town I lived to realize what life was without being raped almost every night. Oh, after that, I was like I want to live, I just don't want to live like that. To this day, I don't ever want to commit suicide, and I want to live life and life it good.

The Greatest Depression: Part Two

This poem is about the struggle that someone has helping themselves up from a difficult life event, whether it's sickness, lost, grief, mental health struggles, financial struggle etc. What do you do? I think we dig deep inside ourselves, and choose to never give up, if we have to go it alone, or do it with help. Don't give up on you, you need you, the world needs you.

Locked Up

I remember always thinking while all this evil was being done to me, "this had to be how it was to be a slave, day after day hoping you don't get raped by your slave master. Locked up the poem is my interpretation of slavery, prison, while being a pre-teen and teenager.

Tearless

There were nights, I had nightmares, sometimes I'd cry, other nights no tears. I wanted the pain to stop, I wanted peace.

Unforgotten

This is one of my first pleads with God, saying please tell me, you didn't forget me. Tell me I'm not forgotten by you.

Chapter Two

Then Relationships

A Romantic after Thought

Dear Person of Interest,

How to start?

I love you— wait. I mean—I wasn't supposed to say that part out loud.

You have captured the gates of my heart.

I'm weakened by your sensual touch, and the warm embrace of your words.

I think I've fallen heals over head for you, and I've landed in your arms.

But I can't tell because my heads spinning, and eyes are closed.

I guess I'm asking you not to let go.

Hold onto me and love me, here in loves sweet serenity.

I know you can't stay forever, but I don't want this to end.

So, I'm pleading with my senses to give in.

Give into your touch, give into your strong and powerful embrace.

Give into your smile, your eyes—man those eyes.

Give into our scent, and into every sacred time spent.

I love you—I mean it.

I've just been too scared to admit it.

So, I wrote it down and sent it to you.

I hope you get this.

Sincerely,

A Second Chance at Us

Creeps that crawl

Something creeps into my heart when you're around.
Something tells me that it's okay, go ahead let your guards down.
Something tells me "I'll always have you around."
Then suddenly you're gone as quickly as I fell for you.

It's funny how we can make up our faces,
but we can't make up our life or lives.
I wonder why I ever listened to the words you whispered in my ears?
Why did I ever put your number in my phone?
Why did I ever care?

Then I remember that you told me to come back to town.
Now I'll never get back those years.
Then I remember you would hide your bitterness,
And I couldn't find it behind your fictitious smile.
Were you ever kind to me or was that also a lie?

I miss the days you pretended to love me
Even though you never meant it.
It meant I wasn't lonely.
It took me so long to find out that all your "hellos' really meant "good-bye."
Now each time I see you, I regret our first "Hi."
As I look forward to another good-bye.

At the Well

At the well of my life is ample water to last an eternity. The water is sweet. Memories of my laughter there at that well. I would sing my favorite hymns as I knelt to catch the cold well water into small slender water bowl. I stopped digging there, instead I began to catch my water at the well nearby. The one after the purple flower bush, adjacent the flat dark grey rock that looks like a tabletop. This is where I dig for water now, and the water there is not plenty. That well is difficult to reach, and the right part of its mouth is slightly caved in. It's not the best well, but it has become the familiar well. When I place my water bowls

down, carefully dropping each
hoping to retrieve enough
My duty to us, after you I
dug there, so I did. I can recall
refreshing well water, I once
do too. At times I would think
other part of that well's mouth
Thus, leaving us nowhere to go,
waters. That well never did fall
our families gathering water at
a well you and I once knew.
beyond our eyes reach. Then
light hearted and fill with a joy.
from their hearts. And I knew
well water renewed them,
moved their thirst. It fulfilled
them like nothing else could.

water bowl inside the well
water for our family to drink.
became one. Once more you
missing the taste of that
knew. Still you dig here, so I
to myself, I hope that the
would collapse into itself.
but back to the sweet heavenly
apart. Remember us watching
the well? A well, I once knew,
They would go down the path
they would reappear laughing,
A joy that seemed to beam
why. I knew that heavenly
transformed them, and re-
their needs and replenished
Their spirits were changed.

That delish well water restored them in ways our well water could never satisfy us. There are moments when I want with all my heart to go back to our fathers, fathers, fathers, fathers well. Yet, I know that means I must leave you. So, I am returning to the well that holds eternity in every droplet of water. Back to the water that gives plenty, more than my water bowls can sometimes hold. Back to my well, back to the well that never runs dry. I am returning to the well that fills me up, to the well that gives me joy and laughter. Here I am at the well. Well, I return to you. I'm at the well where you and I met.

Broken Hearted

I remember the moment we parted.
I told you it was over, but I stilled loved you, you still loved me.

I cried, you cried, we cried in each other arms.
I wiped your tears, and you cried on me.

I held you,
but then we had to let go.

I remember our first kiss, cheek.
There was love in what we had I know it, it couldn't have all been fake.

Didn't we care for each other?
I knew your mother and father, and you knew mine.

Didn't we have a baby?
Didn't you ask me to marry you?

But now I am standing here, broken hearted.
Broken hearted without you, without me.

Broken hearted, by myself.
Broken hearted, but not broken.

FIX*ated*

I used to think I loved you.
But the more I think about how felt about you.
The more I realize that I didn't.

I see now that you are part of a lust filled sea.
What I had for you was nothing close to what love has meant to me.
We were friends though in my mind it was always complicated.

Infatuated with what could be, No longer was I focused on what I could be.
Fixated on what we should be, I turned couldn't, into could be.

I wanted more than I could handle.
More than you could give me.
The friend you were, and now I wish you would have stayed that way.

You told me you weren't ready,
but I was fixated on what we could be.
Engrossed in what I wanted us to be.

Infatuated with what could be, no longer was I focused on what I could be.
Fixated on what we should be, I turned couldn't, into could be.

All I knew was your voice sounded like a voice telling me you loved me.
But the truth is you were the voice telling me you couldn't love me.
So many should nots turned into imaginary should bees.

How could you?
How could you not be in love with me?
I was in love with you, or so I thought.

Infatuated with what could be, no longer was I focused on what I could be.
Fixated on what we should be, I turned couldn't, into could be.

Were you ever in love with me?
Or was it just have lust you had for me?
I mean—how could I have not seen you for who you were not?

You couldn't give me what needed.
And the more you couldn't, the more I gave you, and the more you took from me.
Until I looked into your eyes, and I saw you had nothing more to give.

Infatuated with what could be, no longer was I focused on what I could be.
Fixated on what we should be, I turned couldn't, into could be.

You couldn't give me more.
Mad, I spent almost a decade comparing every man to you,
Young me wishing and wanting you, only to never have you.

Even in arms reach I couldn't have you.
If I could only take you in my arms, to hold, to touch, I would grasp you.
But I couldn't have and hold you in holy matrimony.

Infatuated with what could be, no longer was I focused on what I could be.
Fixated on what we should be, I turned couldn't, into could be.

So, I've concluded you were never meant for me to have.
And this fixation has been an obstacle in my path.
Why do I want someone that had never wanted me?

I get nauseating in my stomach thinking of you.
The thought of you use to make me cry, all those sleepless nights.
I remember knowing I could never have you by my side—I'd pity myself.

Infatuated with what could be, no longer was I focused on what I could be.
Fixated on what we should be, I turned couldn't, into could be.

But now I refuse to lose myself another year,
This has gone on for too long—this must end.
Fixation, I'm done. Done.

You say I run, but this time I will not run.
Only walk to you and stand here to tell you that "IT'S OVER."
As I walk away from you I'M OVER YOU.

"X"

Thinking of you, thinking of our
spent together. Ever kiss, we kissed,
Pain I caused you, pain you caused
like you are always on my mind.
someone new, my mind is on you?
differently. Now, I started to move
I kiss different, dress different, you
you but minute the scent of what we
your arm for protection. Hoping you
you didn't hold me up anymore. You
Finally, I let go of you. It wasn't easy.

then. Thinking about all the time we
every hug, every embrace. Every pain.
me. If only I could let you go. It seems
Why? Why is it that when I'm with
I think about how I would do things
differently. I hug less. I think differently,
are not here and your still affect me. I left
once were still lingers. I once held onto
could protect me I held you tightly. Until
let go of us, you only had room for you.
But it was necessary. We needed to end,

we are finish.
We may have agreed at one point
that we were meant to be, but now we
both see we were both wrong. In this
new season your position in my life
has changed I has changed. I am no
longer the woman that loved you.

I am the woman who finally
love herself, love the one who
loved you. I've learned that my
belongs to my Lord. The Lord
Lord who has called me and
almost lost my heart to you.
you did not know me. Didn't
love. The love of God from
love to be perfected, but it
to have. I was never yours
So, I let you go and you
was meant to be. Now I
signs that lead me away
me peace. I have a better
Me with Love. God's love
go. A love that springs
humility. My heart is
Heart strong. To my
my hearts song.
in endings

has love. A woman who is learning to
gave her the heart. This heart that once
heart doesn't belong me or you. It only
of my heart, the Lord of my life. The
calls me daily. I remember when I
I almost lost my life to you. You,
know that I needed to see true
me. If only we waited for our
never did. You were not mine
to hold in sickness or death.
let go of me. The end of us
see clearer than ever the exit
from you. Leaving you gave
understanding of what love is.
for me. A love I will never let
forth joy, peace, patience, and
learning love. Heart smart.
hearts Creator I am learning
heart's creator. Now I see that
newness arises.

SILENT TREATMENT

You don't have to hold me, for me to know you long for my touch.
You don't have to smile or look my way, for me to know you still love me.
You don't have to kiss my lips, for me to know you wish you could.

You don't even have to breathe in my direction,
Mad or not, I know all the little crazy things you do.

I know you're mad when you pull the sheets,
By the loud thunder of your angry feet.
You breathe heavy when you're mad at me.

You skip words, misspell when you write.
When you're mad, your rhymes don't rhyme right.

You're ugly, when you think I don't know,
You give me the silent treatment,
But I should be giving it to you.

Your lies seep through your skin.
I'm done putting up with your dirty lying ways.

You've violated, and manipulated me,
And I've been too dedicated to you all this time.
I've given you all of me, even all my money.

Counting it the names of other women in my face,
Mad because I will no longer chase you.

I'm done with you—I can't take your lying anywhere.
Not even a robber would claim you.
How did I ever stay and justify the crazy things you would do?

How can I stay with you? You, who would lend yourself to everyone but me.
I am finished with you.

Beaten, Bruised, Bewitched

Missed Birthdays and Anniversaries.
Day after day without love or warmth.

Tomorrow's regrets,
Yesterday's fret.
Today's heart pains leak blood from my chest down to my feet.
Your seductive words buckle my cartilage making it hard to retreat.

Your words send signals to my brain telling me this is it.
Slowly my feelings take over and my brain believes the story you tell.

Our love story is like roses with hidden thorns.
Your kisses blinded side my better judgment.
It's so wrong, but a part of this feels right.
So, I stay here under your naked body, thinking that it can work.

And before I fall for you, my heart remembers the stories of old.
Now I'm trying to rationalize should I leave, or should I stay?

Years of pushing away good advice.
Years of settling for men with bad vices.
Where did I go wrong?
Something isn't right, but it's been wrong for so long.

Now your kisses on my face are to hide your newly thrown blows.
Lies, and hidden agendas wrapped up in tiny pretty bows.

Laughter turned into tears,
Anticipation, excitement turned into apprehension and fear.
I try to forget the blade that was held at my neck.
Because with you, I don't know what's next.

Feelings of guilt, dishonor from those dreadful relationships, agonizing sorrow,
Memories seek to challenge a hope for beautiful tomorrow.

Corners

Seaton, Bewitched

I wish I could see you for who you really are.
Instead, I see this shining ball.
I look at you like a treat to a trained dog.
And all you had to do is show an ounce of interest in me to have me.
I was desperate for love,
So, I took anything that came to me even though I knew it wasn't right.

Oh' how I wish I could see all of you,
You who took no time to know me.
Me, who just saw you as an alluring light.
Oh' I wish I could hear you, instead I hear the silence of my empty rooms,
No footsteps, no laughter, no family, no you coming home hungry after work.
Just me waiting for you to fall in love with me.

I wanted a you,
I wanted a relationship whether it was good and bad.
I wanted it so bad, I lost everything I had.
I was willing to lose me over, and over again to have you.
You who I didn't know—but I wanted you to be part of my life.
You who didn't know, that I was dreaming up a future for us

I thought time would reveal that you were just right for me.
I wanted you, to have you, to hold you, to marry you.
If only in my disillusion I was willing to see you for you.
The fact is not knowing the corners of you, was my wrong turn.
I turned the wrong corner, bumped into you, and lost my identity.
Should I have known from the start—that you and I was a mental mirage?

I wish I knew your corners before I hung you up on the wall of my heart.
Fact is I don't know all the corners of you.
For years I've only known the parts you showed me.
I wish I would have seen through you from the start.
But there are far too many days, and years of wasted time.
Far too much wasted time waiting.

I cannot spend any more time on you, wishing I could understand you.
Staring at the corners of your eyes, trying to look at the corners of your mind.
I wanted your sides to match up to who I wished for.
It was wasted time, time wasted, time invested, and now time lost.
As I somberly recall the myriad mirage of us, I see it was a hopeless dream.
I have a new perspective of this thing, I no longer want you or your corners.

Forget

I wish I could tear out all the pages of these bad memories.
I wish, I wish my past was filled with Love and goodness.
I wish I could remove the offenses and embarrassments.

Forget every tear, every hurt, every hit, ever smack.
Forget every thrust against the wall, as I prayed for my next breath.
Forget the palms of his hands griping the round of my neck.

Forget every "I love you…"
Forget every "I'm sorry, please forgive me."
Forget every "I didn't mean it…"

Every "…you know I get upset sometimes."
Every make-up session we had, while tears flowed from my eyes.
Every "Sorry baby" smile.

Every "You can't let your family see you like this…"
Every "Please don't leave, I can't live without you"
Every kissed drenched in lies.

Forget every time I let you touch me
like a husband would his wife.
Except a good husband would never to try to kill his wife.

I wish I could rip out every page.
I wish I could rip out every page.
I wish I could rip out every page.

I wish I could rip out every page of pain,
and just start all over again.
Oh' I wish I could forget.

You Can't Save Me

I always run to you,
but when are you ever there?
I cry hoping you would hear me, as my heart flies to you,
bursting through the nimbus painted sky.

When all my hope is broken into pieces,
I think you will able to rebuild it.
I immediately dive into your arms,
instantly I end up empty handed.

I wish I could remember the last time you were there for me.
Nothing comes to mind.
I wonder why I always look for you
in my darkest times?

It's as if in the story of my life,
you're the Hero.
But I see now that's not who you are.
I am my own Hero, and it's never been you.

I can't count on you.
You won't catch me. You won't be there.
Even when I want you to.
I'm learning not to trust you.

I'm learning not to depend on you.
Because you won't be there in the end.
You can't save me,
and the fact is you never could.

Love me, don't hurt me

Love don't take me for a ride.
Love don't injure my tender fragile insides.

Love don't leave me far behind.
Love don't erase me from your mind.

Love don't leave my heart dying on the floor.
Love don't let me see you walk out the door.

Love if I lose you where would my hope be?
Love don't lose hope in me.

Love if you don't hold on, who will hold on to me?
Love I'm near-sided and you're all I can see.

Love all I know is you and I are destined to be.
Love I beseech you, reveal yourself to me.

Love — Love me.
Love — Love me if you are for me. If you are what I need.

Whatever you do Love,
Just don't hurt me.

Jade

Jade but not jaded.
I am rare and green.
Young but not mean.

I can be up, and I can be down.
I have a mood, and sometimes it swings.
Jade but not jaded.

I am rare and green.
I am green like jade.
Not green like envy.

Yes, I have moods and sometimes they swing.
I am green like jade.
Jade but not jaded.

What is Love?

What is Love?
I've heard so much about it.
I've heard that it can heal you.
I've heard that it's powerful.

I've heard that it fearless.

I heard it can do anything.
I heard it is without flaw.
I've heard it is not proud, yet it stands tall.
I heard that it is patient, and always astonishingly kind.

I love.

The love for me is inside wonders, where does my love live.
I have heard the thoughts of love echoes in my mind.
Inner thoughts of what love is,
leaves me with questions.

More questions.

When I look outward for love it is grim.
I've heard the worlds view of love is dim.
I've heard the heavenly view of love.
Still I want to know what is Love?

Chapter 2 Breakdown

Chapter Two: Then Relationships

This chapter is all about my Ex-relationships, Ex-crushes, Ex-persons-of-interest, and the relationships that I had with them. I remember after I gave this chapter its title, I thought "I don't want to talk about this again after I finish this chapter (Laugh Out Loud). The reason for that is mainly due these poems being about men I'm no longer interested in. There are great benefits for writing about "The Ex's" as I call them, which is processing (the working out my emotions and thoughts of what was happened in those past relationships). I needed to sort old mindsets out, good habits, bad habits, misplaced feelings, and so much more so writing this chapter was a blessing in disguise.

A Romantic after Thought

This is poem about a guy I dated in college. We attempted to have a relationship, but we didn't fit as a couple. I wrote this poem before I realized that.

Creeps that crawl

Referencing how I've met men who have sweet talked and lied themselves into my life, and how I had no idea what was happening at the time.

At the Well

This poem is about being a woman who has fallen into relationship with a man, who once shared the same faith and beliefs as her. Since becoming married, the man in the relationship has walked away from his faith and she has too.

Broken Hearted

A poem about how relationships, break-ups, and how they start sweet, and flawless, but morphs into something you'd never expect or desire. In the End of every relationship, we decide how we want to end it and leave it.

Fixated

This poem is based on a long-time crush, and kind-of sort of relationship that I lingered in and pined over for almost 10 years. I wrote this poem to work on permanently being over this person, I thought if I could see how much I don't know, maybe I'll why it will never work. Mission successful and we are still friends.

"X"

A poem about how I realized that my past relationships were bleeding into anything new, I tried to start. This was very intentional letting go poem.

Silent Treatment

I almost removed this poem from this book several times, this was a challenge to explore emotionally. Silence is extremely complicated, and more hurtful than I think we give it thought.

Beaten, Bruised, Bewitched

This is my first time writing about domestic violence. My personal experience as a teenager and young adult. It was during college. I had to run away from the home I had with my then fiancé to stay alive and start over.

Corners

This poem is about being honest with myself about what I didn't know about a person of interest. It's also is about allowing myself to let of the fantasy of what "could be."

Forget

Who doesn't want to forget somethings sometimes? Oh, this poem can make me cry at the thought of it, it's my second poem about my personal experience with domestic violence.

You Can't Save Me

I would run into relationships for comfort and companionship. In the beginning of the relationships, we both tried to rescue the other person. I later learned to take ownership of my feelings and the actions my feelings sometimes led me to do.

Love Don't Hurt Me

I remember writing this poem hurting, and thinking I hope love doesn't give me a black eye or bruise my ribs. I don't want to hurt anymore, and it seemed like all my pain included other people. Yet, I haven't given up on a love that doesn't hurt me.

Jade

This poem is written with the premise of not being injured from past relationships. I was so jaded, that green would have envy my shade and color.

What is Love?

I honestly think that Love is the most complex concepts and action ever. I wrote this poem to expound on the thought.

Chapter Three

Working through it

I should have Ran

I should have ran, the moment that he touched me.
Molested me.
Touched my body as if I was a woman, when I was a child.
I should have ran.

I should have ran the first time you said "God said…"
How dare you use God's name, to justify raping me?
I should have ran when he was sleeping.
I SHOULD HAVE RAN.

I should have ran.
I SHOULD HAVE RAN.

I should have and told my brother.
I should have ran.
I should have ran when you terrorized me with pistols and shot guns.
I should have ran when you threatened to kill me.

I should have ran, when I noticed that I could no longer tell my friends the truth.
I should have ran, when friends couldn't come over, and I couldn't leave.
They never knew, but I knew, and for that I should have ran.
I SHOULD HAVE RAN.

I should have ran.
I SHOULD HAVE RAN.

Yes, I was a child.
Still I wonder why I didn't recognize that I should have ran?
I should have ran the first time I tried to kill myself, pills in the eighth grade.
Then I tried to kill myself again, and again, and again, year, after year.

What was I thinking?
A child with no guidance or love.
I was lost. I needed my family, but they weren't there.
I should have ran away.

I should have ran.
I SHOULD HAVE RAN.

I Moved across state, but stayed in a state of shame.
I wanted to break free—a college student looking for new friends and a new life.
I wanted to a new life, but I was struggling to leave a part of that painful past?
Looking back at it now, I was still attached to the death and evil?

All I know is that I SHOULD HAVE RAN. Ran as fast as I could.
I should have ran. I SHOULD HAVE RAN.

Ran until I was out of New York state.
Ran until I fainted, and woke up and ran again.
Over a decade has passed and I still find it hard to love myself,
while thinking that I should have ran.

I realize now that years ago I froze,
And I don't get to hate myself for freezing.
I can love myself. I love myself,
Even though I once thought that I should have ran.

Mad at you God

I hate to admit this,
but the fact is,
       I've lived in part of this lie,
       Afraid and fearing God and fearing for my life.
          Me who buckled at the sound of your voice God, I feared you.
          I wanted so badly to say that I love you,
               but as bad as bad is, there is no love in it.
          I am mad at you God.

So, my bad.
My bad, I thought you left me to die.
       My bad, I thought that all you stood for was a lie.
       My bad, I thought that you had forsaken me.
          Thought that you left me.
          That you abandoned me as tears ran down my eyes.
               I wanted to leave this world and leave you too.

God, why did you leave me?
God, where was your hand?
       Where were you when I couldn't stand?
       When I couldn't stand up for myself?
          Where were you as the world beat me down?
          When everything unholy,
               vile thing was all that could be found in my life?

Where were you God?
Where were you when I prayed?
       Did my prayers not reach you?
       Where were you when I cried?
          Did you not hear my cries?
          Where were you when I said no?
               NO. NO. NO. NO. NO. NO.NO.
               Until I thought No-one could hear me?
                    Until my voice was blocked by his hand?
               Where were you then God?

Where were you when I needed you to save me?
       Where were you God, you said you would never leave or forsake me?

Where were you when I was raped, day after day?
Where were you God?
I'm mad at you God.
I'm mad at you.

I'm mad at you God, I can't see straight.
You were supposed to be my light, but all I saw was darkness.
I'm mad at you, you were supposed to protect me.
Where was your hedge of protection then?
I'm mad at you, you should have made me stronger.
Why wasn't I strong enough to push him off me?
Why wasn't I strong enough to save myself?
Why did you make me so weak?

So weak, that at age nine I couldn't tie a knot strong enough to kill myself,
No one was around, who would have missed me.
So weak, that I couldn't save myself.
So weak, that every day I went on with life.
So weak, that I thought that I could take my own life.
So weak, that I couldn't cut my wrist or stab chest with that knife.

So weak, that I couldn't stand in front of a car to end my life.
So weak, that I couldn't run away,
So weak I couldn't take my life.
But I could run in track practice week after week.

She wasn't the one who raped me, and her kids are nice.
After all, I am the God mother to her grandchild.
Confusion was the pollution, that poisoned my life.
I was weak and foolish, use to being abandoned,
I was young and filled with a deadly poison.
I was WEAK.

So weak, that it took a nervous breakdown,
And a strand of unfortunate events to finally have me tell my older brother,
I was raped for six years in the house we lived in.
Six years too long, because I was weak.

So weak, that I went back to the house that hurt me,
Still weak I would visit with her grandchild, as an adult — weak.
To the home where I was molested, and threatened to kill me,
So weak, that I thought 'she didn't do it, she's fine,
So weak, weak.

So weak that, I sometimes want to curse my Dad, for abandoning me.
Where were you when I needed you the most?
    A Dad who couldn't do a thing for me, but leave.
    So weak, that I can't talk to my mother more than a few minutes,
       And when I do, it's about nothing at all.
           Too weak to try to have more than what we had in the past.
          I was weak.

So weak, that sometimes when I shower,
It's like seeing the rapist looking at me
    That perverted devil.
    So weak, I thought that what happened to me was my truth.
       The only thing I knew was abuse, lies, and plunder.
       I became too weak to change my life,
          I sank in it, and died, and died a thousand times.
          I to hold onto anything that looked like love.

Weak. Weak. Weak.
    Weak, weak, weaker than weak.
    Weaker than weak, I was weak, and you made me this way.
       I am mad at you God.
       I am mad at you God.
          So much that I feel sometimes I hate you.

I wish I was a boy sometimes, they are strong,
I wish I a man, I wouldn't have to be this weak woman.
    I wish I was strong.
    But I am a woman.
       I want to be strong, and not weak.
       But all I can think is you made me like this — A Woman.
          Are all women as weak as me?
          Is this a me a thing? Or a woman thing?
            Being and existing weak?

How can I gain strength, after being so weak?
    How can strong come from me?
       How can I be stronger?
          How can I no longer be weak?
          How can I be strong?
            Strong. Stronger.

I don't want to be mad at you.
I don't want to hate you.
I don't want to fight you.
I want to love you.
Because I know you love me.
Even though you made me weak.,
Even though you made me woman.

I'm mad at you God,
But I'm mad at me too.
Because I had so many chances to run, and I didn't.
I could have saved myself, But I didn't.
Just stayed there dying, every day lying, every day crying.
Crying, crying, crying, crying, dying, lying, crying.
God, you could have saved me, but you didn't.
So, I'm mad at you God.

I wish I was better than this.
But how can someone like me be Great?
How can someone so weak do anything great with her life?
How can someone so weak ever make a difference in life?
How can someone so weak ever choose life, and not death?
How can I be strong, when I feel I have nothing left?

I'm mad at you God.
I'm mad at you God.
And the truth is you're probably mad at me too.
You make me sad and it's true.
And I probably make you sad too.
But I can't stay mad at you God,

I don't want to be weak, but I was born this way.
Where is my strength? I need you Lord.
Lord I need you to be my strength when I am weak.
Be my strength—because I am woman.
A woman who used to being over powered by abusive men?
Where are you Lord?
Where is my strength?

Then I hear an answer:

I hear the Lord saying,
You are not alone.
I am here.
You are my child.
Do not fear.
I have you in the palm of my hands

My response:

Lord—I waited.
Lord—I prayed, but you never came.
Lord—You let him rape me.
Lord remember when they tried to kill me?
Where were you then?

Several Years Later:

But Lord, I will cease to disrespect and hate you for all the evil done to me.
Being mad at you Lord has become too much for me.
I want to let go of being mad at you.
I want to let go of hating you, and blaming you.
I want to stop being mad at you God.
I want to let go.
I'm ready to let go.
Let go of being mad at God.

Now I know:

Yes, Women are strong.
No, Women are not being who are weak.
Yes, Women our essence is strength.
The presence of a woman is strength she is not a weak vessel.
How can I be strong?
I am strong.
I am a strong woman.
Strong. Stronger.

Forgive Myself

I hold onto the hate,
I turn it all inward and aim at myself.
Instead of forgiving myself,
I hate. I hate, I hate me.

Me who let someone rape me for years.
Me who did not tell a soul that I was molested and raped.
Me who reported it just a few years
shy of the time they could make an arrest.

I don't forgive me.
I don't forgive me for all the things that someone did to me.
All the times I was forced to have sex with a grown man,
While still a child teenager, I hated me.

I hated me for not running.
I hated me for not loving me.
I hated me for not forgiving me.
So, I held on.

I held on to the past.
I don't let go of things that hold me bound.
I do my best to give it all to God, but all I do is hate me.
I wish I could forgive me.

But I,
I was holding onto all the things I should let go.
I've wanted so much to love myself,
But my heart and my mind say 'NO'!

NO—you betrayed us,
NO—you worked with the enemy.
NO—you let him rape you.
NO—you let him hurt you.

NO—you let him molest you.
NO—you didn't tell your parents.
NO—you didn't tell the cops soon enough.
NO—you let us die in that house—silent and hurt and as a mute as a rock.

NO.
NO.
NO.
You don't get be forgiven.

No.
You betrayed me,
You betrayed us.
You betrayed yourself.

No.
No.
NO, to love.
NO, to peace.

No.
NO.
You don't get to be forgiven.
NO, You get nothing.

Lord Am I Acceptable?

Lord, you said you would never leave me.
But does that mean that I never disappoint you?
What does your love look like when you don't agree with my life choices?
Do you cry when you see me confused?

Do you care when you see me holding onto the world more than you?
Do you cry when you see me hurt myself unknowingly?
Lord, do you love me when I'm not who you want me to be?
Lord do you love me when I don't think I'm acceptable for you?

When I don't distinguish who I was created to be?
Where does your love go then?
When I sin, does your love hide its face from me?
When I curse you, does it leave me completely?

When I commit adultery? When I covet? When I lie?
When I execute my enemies with my hands or in my thoughts?
Are you there in my darkest hour?
Lord do you love me then?

Lord does your love hide?
What if I question my sexuality?
When I think that I should have been a man not a woman?
Where does your love go then? Lord does your love leave me?

Where does your love go when I'm not what society says I should be?
Who should I be? Who do you want me to be Lord?
Lord where does your love go, when I'm not woman enough?
Lord where does your love go, when I'm not man enough?

Am I not Irish enough? Am I not Black enough?
Am I 'lit' enough? Am I enough?
Is my hair curly enough, is it straight enough?
Is this the right dress, shoe, shirt, pants? Is how I dress enough?

When I feel I'm not, am I enough?
Lord, am I ever enough for you?

Am I tough enough? Strong enough?
Am I loud enough? Am I bold enough?

Am I smart enough?
Am I rich enough?
Am I down enough?
Am I cool enough?

Not creative enough?
Not confident enough?
When is who I am ever enough for you Lord?
Lord when I question you, do you still love me?

Lord, how come I can't hear you?
Lord, where is your warm embrace?
Lord am I so evil, and horrible, so not enough for you?
That you hide your face from me?

When do my actions please you?
Must I always do everything by the book?
Everything?
I know it's right, it just sometimes I don't know enough?

Must I do everything right, even when you don't look?
Must I do everything right, even if everyone else is does what's wrong?
Must I? Should I always follow you?
Would my obedience be an acceptable offering for you?

Do you desire more from me?
What is enough for you Lord?
When am I acceptable for you Lord?
How can I be acceptable for you Lord?

Lord tell me, how can I be enough for you?
What is enough for you?
Lord am I enough for you?
Am I acceptable?

Wrongfully accused

AAAAAAHHHHHhhhh,
I BLAME YOU.
AAAAHHHhhhh.
I blamed you for all of it.

All of it, it had to be you.
All my pain, all my hurt.
Every bruise, every cut, every hit.
Every punch to my stomach.

Every empty stomach growing up as a child. Did no one care for me?
AAAAAaaahhhhh, YOU.
You, you let this happen to me.
I know you, you knew.

You had to have known this would happen.
You know everything and see everything.
You could have stopped it. You could have stopped all of it.
Don't be surprised if I'm mad at you.

STOP!
WAIT—IT WASN'T HIM.
It was the other guy.
WHAT?

WHAT? —Yes, you know the one who's always trying to kill you,
Terminate you and your future.
You've mistaken him for the one who said, He knows the plans for your life.
They are not the same. Not at all.

He has been wrongfully accused,
And you've been mad at the wrong person.
Don't you see all the good in your life, that was the one with the plan?
See the abuse, hurt, death, that was the one who kills, steals and destroys.

You know the one with a plan, has all power,
But wasn't it the one with the plans doing to have me suffer?
Was I ever meant to have better?
Remember wanting to tell my guidance counselor and school nurse?

That was the one with all power speaking—He understands why you didn't.

You wanted to every day,
You would ask to go to the guidance counselor to talk,
And then once there you would talk about some unrelated.
I know it hurts, I know you hurt, I know this all hurts.

Look at what you've overcome.
I know at times it looks like a past filled with neglect.
But the truth is, it's a past filled with strength.
You are a conquer, you've triumphed over the most difficult parts of life.

Look deeper, look at what you have on inside of you.
You may not want to hear this, but God does love you.
God has not forgot you, and He is the one with the plan for your life.
Not thoughts of evil, but of health and an expected end.

Look deeper, please look again.
He's never left your side. Look now, He is still there.
He will never leave you alone.
You are His child, heir to His throne.

Wrongfully accused of not loving you, wrongfully accused of forsaking you.

Forgive and let go of the blame toward God.
God is for you. God loves you.
He is not your enemy,
God loves you. Yes, He loves me.

Chasing Clouds, Not Bad Dreams

Running into puddles, baking mud pies with every type of dirt I could find.
Looking at the world like it was mine.
Thinking I could do anything that I imagined.
I imagined it all.

Skipping on top the clouds.
Leaping from continent to continent.
My pencil was the beginning of my everywhere.
I could be in Afrika, then Ireland, or a small island off the Australian coastline.

In the deep of the sea swimming with the great humpback whale.
Or swimming with a deadly shark.
I was everywhere, with one thought, and one pencil.
Then lost my innocence at the one wrong time.

I began to see life through stained and blurred lens.
I couldn't see a thing. I was Blind.
I couldn't do anything. I was stuck.
Life left me weary, my troubles turned me to stone.

I no longer moved through life filled with hope.
I didn't believe anymore.
I just stood still in my disbelief.
I was frozen in the lies of my past life.

Losing grasp of my beautiful dreams,
Faster than they could grow, the were uprooted.
I didn't know how to get my dreams back,
But I knew I had lost it.

Something in me was sleeping.
Something inside of me needed to be awaken.
Something inside of me needed to be alive.
Instead I was slowly and silently dying.

I know it was the trick of the Devil that came to take my life.
The Devil made living seem so unappealing—A lie that I began to believe.
The devil made love looked like a life of strife—Another lie not worth believing.
My innocent bright brown eyes did not suddenly lose hope one day.

It was the Prince of Darkness, who stole my joy, hopes, and dreams.
But it was God who gave me my joy again, God who gave me my peace.
God who returned my zeal for life and gave me love
and a renewed a mind filled new dreams.

I am so grateful that God has never left my side.
Because now I can run, jump and leap as I dance my pain out.
Sing and shout my pain out.
Write and paint my pain out of memories lodged within my faith.

The days that I cry, I cry and cry my pain out.
I'm using what God gave me to rebuild myself and as my Redeemer rebuild my life.
I'm using my Heavenly Fathers love to heal me—Lord thank you for healing me.
With the help of God sent people, family and friends, I can see me again.

Now I have hope, and now I am moving.
With resilience I refuse to stay down.
I am believing again, no longer standing frozen.
Now I'm chasing clouds, no more bad dreams.

Four Walls

Four walls have been holding me at night.
Four walls have been listening ears that I could not find in a friend.
Four walls have been shoulders to cry on,
as tears flow from my heart and hit the floor.

Four walls have been keeping me.
Four walls have been home.
Four walls safely holding back the wind and rain from me.
It's warm in the winter inside four walls.

These four walls are sometimes like a dungeon to me.
Four walls like a punishment never letting me go.
Four walls like a prison.
Though in this prison there are windows, a front door, and I hold the keys.

Four walls holding me back from the world
Four walls after work, four walls after school,
Four walls became the next thing to do.
Four walls like an invitation to another night at home alone.

A date with four walls.
Four Walls keep me from excepting invitations.
Four Walls for you I'm cancelling plans and rejecting new ones.
When I want to be alone with my thoughts I can turn to you Four Walls.

Four walls became an alibi.
Four walls and I.
Four walls become my scapegoat.
Four walls keeping me from being who I am supposed to be.

Four Walls,
How can I blame you?
All you were meant to do was stand,
And be four walls.

Dear God, I need a Mommie

I wish I had a Mother who cared for me.
Was there for me.
Would give up the whole world for me.

I wish I had a Mommie.
I wish I had a Mommie.

I wish I had a Mommie who woke me up, put clothes on me,
Braided and brushed my hair.
She'd fill up my tummy with food.

Stuff me with love and hugged me.
Then would send me off to school.

But my Mommie isn't here.
My Mommie is all the way over there.
Mommie let me leave her, her there and me here.

Where is my Mommie?
Where is my Mommie?

I wish I had a Mommie that told me she loved me,
I wish I had a Mommie that told me she loved me,
I wish I had a Mommie that I could run to.

A Mommie whose voice I knew, and wouldn't run away from,
Because she didn't finish raising me.

I wish I had a Mommie.
I wish I had a Mommie.
I wish I had a—

I wish I had a Mommie that was here,
I wish I had a Mommie that was here.

I wish I had a Mommie that I could run to.
To run into her arms,
and hear her say I am here.

Proud of me

For years, I hoped that my father would notice me.
Notice how great I was doing in school.
Notice how I didn't get in trouble.
Notice that I was home, and he wasn't. How that was wrong,

But he didn't.

I guess you can say I have a father complex.
I guess you could say I have a defect.
I guess, I'm stuck on "proud of you"
I never heard it as a child, "I'm proud of you daughter."

They say it makes you look for attention in all the wrong places, like men.

So, I'm all grown up sleeping in arms.
Arms of a man who could never love me the way a father could.
The way a father should.
Honestly, I never wanted them to.
I never wanted a man to replace you—my father.

I only wanted you, my father.

Years of wishing you could see me.
Hoping when I have my first child, they won't witness our brokenness
Hoping they don't notice their Mother is hurting, unloved by her father.
The Grandfather they've grown to know, who loves them. They'd never understand.

All I wanted was my father to like me, to love me, to want me, need me.
All I wanted was my father to be proud of me.

Tell me am I loved?
Tell me I'm the daughter you wanted?
Tell me you are happy you had me?
Tell me I'm the dream you had that finally came to fruition.

Tell me you're "proud of me."
I'm waiting.

No Dad, No Daddy, No Father

I had no Dad I could brag about.
But my Daddy in Heaven says, love is not braggadocios.
Perhaps it was for the best.
No Dad that would tuck me into bed like they did in the movies.
No Dad to watch movies with.
No, I was invisible to my dad. I was never the apple of his eyes.

My Dad didn't make me feel special.
Nor did he teach me things about life that I needed to know.
Nor did we have our own silly sayings, that only we understood.
I never had a Daddy that laughed with me,
Instead he'd laugh at me.
When I was a child, I thought my dad hated me.

No Dad, No Daddy, No Father.
Just me, my Daddy—My Heavenly Father.

Didn't have a Daddy that taught me how persevere and show up.
When he gave me up, that taught me how to give up.
Then it taught me how to fight.
I didn't have a Dad, Daddy, or a Father, only a man I rarely saw as a child.
Yet he would wonder if my grades were on track.
Sometimes I wonder what I did to him, for him not to love me?

I call him "Dad," because I fear God, and I honor God by honoring him.
I suppose he is my daddy, because I'm his blood baby.
I didn't have a Father to father me.
I didn't have a Father to call on, or a Father to be my protector.
I had no covering from my him—my Dad.
Why he couldn't take care of me, I don't know?

No Dad, No Daddy, No Father.
Just me, my Daddy—My Heavenly Father.

A Good Daughter

I remember hoping that you would see me.
That you would come home and tell me "good job."
Instead, you would take the belt to me when I did nothing.
Was I ever your good daughter?

Didn't you want me?
I couldn't have birthed me, you helped to make me.
Then you left me.
Wasn't I a good daughter?

Straight A's, did you ever see them?
Did you know what I did in the school play?
My teachers would have loved to meet you — parent-teacher meeting.
Check the paper, I am a good daughter.

Wasn't the fact that you got no bad reports, good for you?
Didn't my smile, make you want to smile too?
Isn't a daughter supposed to be the apple of her fathers' eye?
Was I ever a good daughter?

Went to college, no encouragement from you.
Then did it again without you.
You still don't notice me.
Aren't I a good daughter?

NO CREDIT

When people meet me they say,
Your parents must have raised you well.
Then I say No, not the fact.
I was raised by God.
So, I was raised well by one Parent.

He has shown me where to place my feet, and where not to go.
He has taught me how to read, write, sing, dance, and have joy.
He has raised me, and taught me,
He protects me, he has trampled on the heads of my enemies,
He has given me a voice and a platform to use that voice.

I give no credit to my parents after seven years of raising me.
I give no credit to the guardians my father gave me to.
No credit to his choose in character and people.
No credit to the guardian that raped me, or the other that stood by frivolously,
Elementary, Middle and Highschool I have no one to give credit to.

Yes, I was raised well.
Thank you, Abba.
Thank you, Heavenly Father for being such a good daddy.
But to who you may think, I give no credit.
God has raised me.

Wiser

I have been tricked, fooled, lied to.
In other words, I was taken for a ride, I was life's fool.
The people in my life wanted to take everything from me.
Evil wanted to take my innocence, health, and mental resilience.
In my past there was always someone trying to kill me.
Abandonment tried to kill me, neglect tried kill me, rape tried to kill me.
I avoid missed the end of a sharp blade, but I've avoided death.
Death has no hold of me anymore, and at death is nothing to fear.

This is my wiser.

Now I live in the light, and I no longer live in the darkness.
Wiser than I've ever been, now today I stand wiser.
Waiting for life to hand me something it thinks will break me.
Now I look at life in its' eyes, and say,
I learned to bend so you can't break me.
I've heard it said, "they thought they could kill me by burying me,
Now I see that everything that was against me was for my good.

This is my wiser.

This growth in pain is my wiser.
This peace is my wisdom.
Knowing now, that my life is worth living.
Knowing that my life is worth fighting for.
Worth wisdom's wings stretched across the sky of my once dreary existence.
I am worthy of the chance to breathe a new each day.
I deserve to be my very best, and I deserve a good life.

This is my wiser.

STAY

There's a voice in my mine telling me to stay.
Stay because my body needs me to.
Stay because others need me,
Stay because I have a purpose here,
Stay because God brought me here.

Stay for my unseen purpose.
Stay because of my un-birthed dream.
Stay because—I'll travel when it's time.
Stay because someone else needs me.
But sometimes stay means, you stay in the prison of your mind.

Stay, it can hold you back.
Stay, it can keep you trapped.
Stay, it can leave you blind,
Stay, it can make you crippled.
Stay can tear you apart.
Stay can kill your hopes.
Stay can steal the beat from your heart.

Stay inside if you don't want to be sun burned.
Stay inside to hide from danger.
Stay inside to hide from rejection.
Stay inside to hide from yourself.

But sometimes stay means, you stay in the prison of your mind.
Stay, but help can't ever get there.
Stay, in the burdens of all the evil thoughts, and the ways of yesterday,
Stay in the pain this stay whispers in my ear.
Stay in the desperate depressed, wayward ways.

Why?
Why stay when Jesus is calling you out?
Calling you out.
Calling you out of Bondage.

Out from the strongholds.
Out from the shame.
Out from the guilt.
Out from the fear and the doubt.
Out from that desolate and dry place.
Out from the darkness and into the light.
Out from the mind telling you to run and to hide.
Out of you mind telling you, you've already lost—why try?

Stay and fight.
Stay and watch God fight.
Stay and fight.
Stay and watch God fight for you.
Stay and win, and win, and win, and win again.
Stay and make this stay worth it.
Stay to watch God win for you.
Stay to STAND OUT and be CALLED OUT.

Who Can save me?

I think about you saving me from myself.
Saving me from thoughts of being alone forever, and from this world
I think of you rescuing me from harm and pain.

I think about how strong you are, and how strong I am not.
I think about how stronger if you were near me.
Am I only strong when I'm near you?

I think about you saving me as if you are all I've got.
But when I need saving I know that you cannot.
So, who will save me?

I will save me from harm, pain, fear, doubt and shame.
I will save me from all my troubles.
I can save me, me—I will.

Feelings

I used to hide my feelings.
I remember being beneath the things I loved, or feared, or despised, or confused me.
I feared that getting close to the edge of my mind I would sink.

I would sink into what I am not sure of.
I would sink into the ideas of the past.
I would sink into ideas of the future.

Now I'm wondering how the what's would materialize?
Why the who's of my life were placed there?
Remembering all my mistakes that takes me from high to low.

I saw myself losing track of memories misplaced.
Forgetting the good memories, and the happy moments in life.
But remembering all the sad ones, the bad ones, the ones that want to make me mad.

I used to think that my feelings were running away from me.
I didn't mind those forgotten memories, and the thoughts that would haunt me.
I didn't mind until my feelings started to hurt me, steal from me, and almost killed me.

I never knew how powerful feelings were.
How they could tear me apart if I didn't give myself time to understand them.
Feelings, like a plow machine out of control, tearing up everything in its path with no remorse, nor direction.

Feelings tell me, I am nothing and no one.
Feeling whispering to my insecurities.
Until I silenced them with the truth.

Feelings you don't rule over me, this is not a place to run free, though you can be free to run.
Feelings I carry you, you don't carry me.
Feelings your presence in my life has been a point of contention.

Now I'm over-joyed that things between us has changed—feelings.
Now feelings—thank you for teaching me how to grow.
Now feelings—you have taught me how to handle my pain.

Feelings, you and I have finally arrived.
Feelings, we have arrived at a place where we understand each other.
Feelings, I think I can tell you this—feelings I am not moved by you, I move you.

Body

When I look down, I see a body that has been used.
Ripped open and abused.
A body not used for the glory of God.
Instead for the desires of evil and malicious men.
Hands that violated me, a body that broke me.

As I got older there were ones who didn't know how to love me.
Another man that never wanted me, but they wanted my body.
All used my body to take what they wanted from me.
I let them, I wanted it too, or so I thought,
until I didn't—and then he was mad.

A body used by boyfriends, and by the enemy.
A body that wasn't valued as a body of a friend or a lover.
Men who only wanted my body, and I wanted the same.
I stopped caring about who I shared my body with,
And I lost value in body.

Men who told me they loved me,
But couldn't wait to remove the clothes off me.
But what did I do? Wasn't this my body?
Old enough to do the act, but not emotionally ready.
Yes, it was up to me to say no?

Yes, it was my body to agree or disagree with the actions done to it.
Yet, it wasn't my choice to have it violated, again, and again as a youth.
It was me who laid under him, as he violently held me down.
Me who let my body rest, after struggling to push him off my body.
Me, kicking, screaming, yet nothing I did made the difference at the time.

Me who stayed in my first relationship after running away.
An abusive childhood, to an abusive relationship.
He controlled me, he hit me, he chocked me, my body was abused.
Controlled me until, I could no longer live as—puppet.
I refused to be held in chains by him—puppet master.

I lost the innocence that comes with having an untouched body.
I lost that innocence and died, I cried.
Cried wondering how my body would react to a knife?
A knife, I thought about running past my neck, then my wrist.
I wanted to die.

Because I had just been violated for the first time.
Because I had just lost ownership to my body.
Or at least that what my body felt.
Broken into pieces, as it was forced to do things it never knew.
Things a child's body should not or would never want to do.

My body, my body you have been through so much.
The arms of my body have done things a child should never do.
I wish I had a childhood of a child my age, in my body.
The lips of my body have betrayed itself,
As it surrendered to the decisions and pining of a child-molester.

My lips were forced across places a child's lips should never know.
These breasts have been touched by hands of a molester and thief.
These hips have been held by a rapist and a molester,
a vile person who thought that sexual touching a child, was God's plan.
A vile person who did vile things to a vulnerable child.

I went to bed, ready to go to school.
Instead day after day, night after night taken advantage of as a child.
I laid in that bed wanting to kill him, for what he made me do.
Wanting to kill myself, for what I was being forced to do.
There is nothing else left of this body. There is nothing else left of that body.

I had to leave that body there.
I had to leave that body of mine there in the past, it was killing me.
Killing me, killing my future body.
Killing me, killing my future body of life.
Jeopardizing my future success in love, freedom, joy, self-respect, and wholeness.

Body dying.
Body dying.
I needed to let you die body, it wasn't because I didn't care.
I needed to let you die body, it was the only way I could live.
Thinking, knowing what I know now, would I hated myself, that I'd take my life?

Body, body growing, body living.
Body living, knowing that it wasn't my fault.

Body dying still wanting to die more.
Body living, knowing that I couldn't have ran fast
enough to get away from his body.

Body, grown now, but still the same body.
Body laying with men who couldn't care for me.
Men who couldn't be there for me.
Didn't know how to love me the way God intended for me to loved.
I so very much needed to be loved the way God loves.

I couldn't love them either.
I didn't know how to.
I couldn't love them either,
I didn't know that my body wasn't theirs to enjoy.
That my body wasn't a requirement of true love.

Love,
Love didn't ask to abuse my body.
Love didn't exploit my body.
Love, didn't ask my body to die quietly,
Instead love healed it.

Like all the times I laid their dying in puddle of disgust, Shame, hate, and guilt.
Where were my senses telling me to protect my body?
Where were my senses telling me to protect my bruised, beaten body?
As I was threatened by death and further brokenness?
Broken Body, Broken Body.

Body surrendering to the hands of someone foreign to it.
Body surrendering to the hands of someone it should have never knew.
Twisted mind, twisted body.
Twisted mind, twisted body into internal and external physical wars,
Wars that a body shouldn't have to endure.

As an adult, longing to be with a body that would love me.
I remember I would lose my heart and mind in my body.
I remember betraying self to belittle my mental
and spiritual body.
Just to be with a body.

Yet I endured now, just as I endured as a teenaged child.
Yes—I endured, my body was mine again.
As I ran from a house that was never a home.

I ran from that house, ran away.
Runaway.

As an adult learning to love my body was difficult.
Body that sang songs of hate, yet cried out for love.
Learning to love my body was difficult.
It sang songs of hope and cried out aching.
Yes—I endured, my body is mine again.

Body I love you,
I need you to hold on, don't give up—please for me this time.
Body I love you, I need you to hold on.
Don't give up—please for me this time.
Body I love you—Please. Body I love you—Please.

Body,
Body,
Please,
Please,
Body, Body.

Love me body, love me.
Love me body, love me.
Love me body, love me.
Love me body, love me.
Love me, please body.

It's me body, it's just me, love me, please body.
It's me body, it's just me, body, I love you, Body I need you to hold on.
Don't give up—please for me this time.
Body, I love you, I need you to hold on.
Don't give up—please for me this time.

When I look down,
I see a body that has been used,
A body used for the glory, the glory of God.
A body used for the glory, the glory of God.
Used to praise, worship, to break chains and break free.

Just hold on

There was a time where I needed to hold you tightly.
It was the only way I would know that you were there.
Calling you daily, empty and lost.
I would fumble through each night desiring only you to give me peace.

I would look to my left and then my right,
And if you weren't there, I would panic in fear.
At times I'd lose faith, my heart, my bones,
and my breath cried for you.

Other times, I wanted nothing to do with you.
Knowing that you were the truth,
I would run in the opposite direction.
Now I want only to run to you.

I've lost faith in you Lord too many times—I need you.
I've given up on your existence more than I can count.
I am tired of running from you, running from what you've called me into.
Now I want to run to you.

Now, I want to know you more.
Now, I want to want you,
Now I want to praise your name as loud as I can.

Yeshua, Messiah, Hosanna, Jesus, Savior, Redeemer, Prince of Peace,
Bread of Life, Living Water, Truth, Light, the Word, Lord, Big Brother!
I don't ever want to lose you.
I don't ever want let you go ever again.

Something for Me

I want to embark on a new journey.
Go somewhere I've never been.
Write the world in poetry and stories.
I want to create a space just for me.
I want to dream dreams and live my dreams.
I want more than the mundane day to day life style.
I want my life to be more than a moment in time.
I know that I gain a new perspective, could see this new world with new eyes mine.
I've always done for everyone but me.
I've had to learn that I am worth my efforts, and I am worth me time.
There's nothing wrong with wanting some me time.
I am worthy of my love and my money.
I deserve to live a life worth living, and this is not a selfish ambition.
This is something for me.

God is Love

God is Love.
NO.
YES.
YES,
God is Love.

What do you mean God is Love?
I mean Love is God. The very being of God is love.
How does that work?
Well then what about my broken heart?
What about the abusive relationships that I fled from?

Where was Love then?
I mean where was God then?
Well, God was Love, and Love was God then.
God is Love, and Love is God.
No. No, I don't except that.

First it was a disagreement.
Then the words got brassier.
Then he slammed me against the wall,
chocked you, you hit your head and fall to the ground.
You remember watching him walk out the house?

Then I got up slowly.
I got up, but couldn't move fast enough to stop him.
Nor did your words come out fast enough.
He hurt you, and he didn't check to see if you were alright.
He didn't help me up, and he didn't apologize.

That evening you cried for hours.
You wanted to call your girlfriends.
Anyone of them would had told you to come to their place stay as long as you needed.
But you thought they'd judge first, then blame you and shame you, so, you didn't call.
And you stayed and stayed.

Morning light breaks through the clouds, and you wake up to an empty house.
No phone call, no "I was wrong," no "I'm sorry I hurt you," text.
Only an empty house void of other life but yours, or so it seemed—but 'You are not alone' in God.
Remember that quiet and soft thought pressed against your mind that said, "You can leave."
You need to leave this place.

You need to leave this man, before it gets worse—Remember?
Yes, I remember.
That was God. That was Love.
Here is Love.

Here is God.
God was telling you and guiding you to safety.

Your Heavenly Father was giving you a way of escape.
God was your escape.
Love was your escape.
Did you call your friend, did you call anyone, no—because the devil lied to you?
No—I stayed until he—until he almost
he almost killed me.

He held me hostage in my own house.
He had a blade pressed against my neck.
That was never Love—I didn't know until it was too late.
This is Never Love, This is Never God.
Never would the God who is Love hold you hostage—Love didn't make you stay, theirs lies did.
Or put a knife to you neck—no not God, no not Love.

That it was a lie.
It was a lie that was used to hold you hostage.
A lie with attempts to kill.
Love is not blind.
Love saw it all, God saw it all.

Love is not blind—Love saw it all.
And Love pleaded with you to leave.
God is not blind—God saw it all.
God pleaded with you to leave.
God Love—Love God wanted you to be safe.
Love helped you leave him, God helped you pack your things and go

It's okay.
It's okay to cry. Cry.
Just don't cry out of guilt.
You didn't know that facade wasn't Love.
You are not to blame—God loves you.

God's loves you,
Love for you from your Heavenly Father did that.
Love did that. God did that.
Love that is God, did that.
God did that. Love did that.

That's what love does—It saves.
It protects—It gives room for truth and life.
So that one day you can see,
God is love.
Love is God.
This is the truth.

Love
Over
Lies

Love

Over
Lies,
I hate the Devil.

Love

Over
Lies,
I'm supposed to.

Love

Over
Lies,
Lies are of the devil and I hate to lie.
Because I know it is an evil spirit.

Love

Over
Lies,
It's the evil spirit of it I hate.

Love

Over
Lies,
Sometimes it's like I forget that my greatest love
should be God and His Son.
A Love that reigns today, yesterday, and forever.
Love.

Under Love

Lies,

I thought God didn't Love me.
I thought God made that very clear,

You left me in the hands of my enemies.

Lies,

Under Love

I thought God had forsaken and forgotten me.
I thought that all things work out for the good
of those who love God— Just not me.

Love

Over
Lies,
I prayed, and plead for my husband,
and I got counterfeits instead.
I told God that there was no way I could survive
or continue life without him—that was a lie.
I Begged for a life to change my life.
Not acknowledging that a life came, lived,
died and rose for me already.
Was I being greedy?

Love

Over
Lies,
If I divide all the Love in my life by all the lies,
the Love is much greater.

30/24
20:80
24/30
80:20
30/30
1
100/100
1
30/12
2.5
12/30
.40
40:60

A great pain covered by an even GREATER LOVE.
Looking at the math,
the painful years do outnumber the good.

So, I choose to look at the good within those years.
I choose to I look forward to the good to come.
I realize that the love of God
is still GREATER THAN all the pain I've experienced.
Love is Greater.

Love

Over
Lies,
I now want to live a life for my Heavenly Father.
I desire to love God.

Love

Over
Lies,
My best cannot measure to yours Lord,
And fort that I am grateful.
I am grateful that my best, you take as offering to you.

Love
Over
Lies.

Love
Over
Lies.

Love
Over
Lies.

Love
Over lies.
It's all I can offer to myself to know that,
LOVE has always been above it all.

Chapter 3 Breakdown

Chapter Three: Working through it

Years after being molested and raped, domestic abuse, I faced guilt, shame, broken-spirit, hate, embarrassment, self-loathing, and anger. There is a gambit of emotions I didn't know of or know how to express. I only knew that they were biproducts of these type horrific life experiences. After I decided I would publish these poems, and not just leave them in my journal, I realized it was going to take time to heal. I needed to live a better life, I had to learn how to live a better life. First, I need to work through some things.

I Should Have Ran

This poem was written in an immense amount of pain and brokenness. I blamed myself for being molested and raped for my so many years, because I all I could think was "I should of have ran."

Mad at you God

Mad at you God is about my Love, hate, love relationship with my Creator. Asking Him, why did I have to endure such heart-breaking childhood and adolescence years? Questioning God's love for me, and wondering what was the connection to my pain and His love for me met? If they met at all. I had questions, more questions than pages, and I needed God to explain Himself to me.

Forgive Myself

No matter how matter how many physiologists, Pastors, loved ones said, "it is not a child's responsibility to take on the fault or blame that they are raped." I blamed myself and I hated myself for it.

Lord Am I Acceptable?

A poem written to question what I have to do, or a person has to do to be loved by God. I wondered how a person was suppose act, think, dress, speak to please God? What do I have to do for God to hear me? What are there rules to praying and believing in God? Do I have to be perfect for God to love me? I think God loves me now, but I wonder sometimes, "Lord, Am I acceptable?"

Wrongfully accused

It wasn't until almost 20 years later, that I realize that I had mistaken God's absence during my childhood and adolescence as His wrath and hate towards me. While I wondered where God was in my life, God was holding me up, when I wanted to feel God's presence, God was speaking to me through His words, friendships, and siblings.

Chasing Clouds, Not Bad Dreams

This poem is about having dreams and losing site of those dream due to life experiences.

Four Walls
Four Walls plays with the idea of being overly acquainted with confined spaces.

Dear God, I need a Mommie
After Leaving Jamaica, I no longer lived with my Mother. I spoke to via phone, and it was seldom. It was hard living in a new country without a Mommie.

Proud of me
I wrote this thinking, have I ever heard my Father say he was proud of me? Why don't I remember my Father telling me he was every satisfied with the work I put into being a good student or a good kid? More importantly, why am I so bother by this as a grown adult?

No Dad, No Daddy, No Father.
This poem is about my relationship with my Father. I loved spending time with my Father, we'd go the beach together and sip on our favorite Jamaican soda. As child my Father was my hero, until he wasn't.

A Good Daughter
This poem is another look at my relationship with my Father, I wanted so badly to be wanted and loved by him. Even after writing this, I'm not sure if words can express the hole that forms in the heart of a girl who has an estranged relationship with her Father.

No Credit
I wrote this poem out of anger. The anger came from adults, teachers, and people in the community giving credit to my parents for raising me so well. I would think I don't live with my parents, no-one is raising me.

Wiser
This poem is about learning and gaining wisdom and knowledge from life experiences.

Stay
I wrote stay while living in Florida over 3 or 4 ears ago, and at the time so much of what I wrote was based on different circumstances. This poem has become more and more relevant in my life, and I've never been happier to stay than I am right now.

Who Can Save Me
After realizing that I cannot depend on a relationship, or a man to save me, I needed to formulate a new plan. I had to step up and do for me what no one else could.

Feelings
This is an important poem to me, because I was honest with myself about why I had a cognizant dissonance within me. When I was a girl being molested, I taught myself to stop feeling. I convinced myself that my feelings would make it hard to survive, that the more I felt, the more I wouldn't be able to bare my dreadful life. That the more I felt, the more I would want to die. So, my feelings and I became estranged until I became an adult and realized, I was still functioning under with the safety precaution.

Body

This is a tough one to explain, not because I can't, it's still a tender and delicate topic.

When I was raped, it was like dying. When we die we leave our body, and our spirit leaves us. I was raped over and over, which is like dying over and over. I was a teenager and I knew death like a bird knows the sky. I didn't know it when I was a teenager, but I had major cognizant dissonance. I wasn't sure how to explain or make sense of any of my life anymore, it was too dark, it was grim, and lonely.

This poem explores that enormous disconnect. Before the poem is complete you get to see the reconciliation between and my body, and I fought to reconnect with myself. (You're still reading, but I want to say thanks for reading.)

Just hold on

After living most of my life in America, being abused, assaulted, in pain, in a depressed state of self-loathing, and being disconnected to myself I was ready to go back to Jamaica. I wanted out of my horrible life in America, I wanted out of my life period. I had to encourage myself to not give up on me, my life, my dreams I had as a child, and the ones I now had as adult.

Something For Me

This was another poem that I considered not sharing, because I thought it would make me sound selfish. At the risk of sounding like I don't care for no-one but myself, I wrote it any way. t's memo to reminding I can live for myself too, I don't have to live for someone else's happiness, or someone else goals all the time. I was giving myself permission to do something for me.

God is Love

This is poem is a conversation with God challenging who he is in my life. For years I've worked through my belief in God, and my reason for believing. I wondered for years, how could God love me, and allow me to experience so much pain in my life?

I had to take a new perspective of what I already knew about God. Then I reread several stories in the Bible to realize that my story is horrible, sounds like some other horrible stories I read. I found out I have similar abuse, heart ache, abandonment of many individuals I read about in the Bible. This helped, the sting of my life hurt a bit less, but I still have my questions.

Love Over Lies

This poem is a conversation with myself, about all the things I couldn't make sense of in my life. I think, I was in therapy when I wrote this, so things were getting clearer. Still struggled to understand how I could ever forget what God allowed me to go through. I wondered honestly love God while still being mad at Him and perplexed by His actions or lack of action in my life? In the poem I used numbers as a method to attempt to understand the positive and negative experiences in my life. Oh, the things I did to try and make sense of something, that may never make sense, lol. I have to say I appreciate my dedication to myself, to put in the work to try to figure it out. Now this is self-love at work, even if it meant creating made up math equations.

Chapter Four

Create your way out

 Writing

I relish running into my thoughts.
I delight in walking along my thoughts with the rhythm of my words.
I elate as I skip in the fields with verbs.
I love looking over the hills of the metaphors that transform lines into life.

Writing atop of horizontal lines in a valley of alliterations.
Writing one thought into my life, as I write another out of my life.

Writing is the blood to my veins.
Writing lines of words on scrolled paper.
Like the highways that run to my heart.
Each written word is an imprint of my love.

Art

Covered with color.
Wrapped in a lyrical verse.
Floating along a riff.
Tuning the strings before the praise I lift goes to heaven.
Moving across the floor elegantly, flipping, jumping into the air.
Capturing the beauty of everything around us,
Art.

Stands in the middle of nowhere and wonders,
And then replies, "I see who you are" then captures it.
Though at times words and pictures do not express.
It is important to share the art we have in our hearts.
Expressions, or an unspoken word.
The sound of a memory—the vision that comes from a thought,
Art.

The melody that repeats
in your mind and your heart.
The joy that swings from tree top to tree top from sun ray.
Beautiful gray skies on a lovely rainy day.
Surges of heat bouncing through the atmosphere,
landing on your supple skin, tinting.
Art.

Loudly listening or the sensation
of beats gliding along your skin,
and off soundwaves.
Quiet, as a secret.
Or a wanting of
more and more.
Art.

Written on papyrus
are ancient stories of our families' ways.
Scrolls rolled up with legacy.
Words create great long lines
on once-blank paper.
Look back at you saying— "Thank you for letting go."
Art.

Living in the space of your creativity,
is your individual artistic exceptional expression.
Pure jubilee.
Thought-provoking,
misinterpreted, uncomfortable,
heartbreaking.
Art.

Gently reminding us who we are.
Created by the Great Creator— Art.
Art, you have always been the expression the world was looking for.

Through you

I lift my hands,
I raise my heart,
I look above to where you're seated.

I move to the beat of love that you designed inside of me.

Through you, I move.
Through you, I breathe.
Through you, I live.

I extend my feet, step, I leap.

I jump
into the air as
if gravity isn't.

I extend my legs from right to left.

Each motion and movement,
Tells me that I am alive, and strong, and capable.
Capable of soaring.

Soaring, soaring above every doubt that lives on the ground.

Every fear that tells me to stay down, that lies horizontal on the earth,
As I soar over it.
I dance.

Learning

I pray to you before the test, I run to you.
I learn by trusting you Lord.
I go to the Creator and say, "I need to pass this, I need your help, I need you."
My experiences sometimes fool me, a memory or a school of thought.

I don't' need to live out every mistake or every scenario.
I've realized that the life of my Mother, isn't what drives my experience. I get to choose.

I'm learning this world is scary at times.
My mind races as I think to myself, "is this the right move?"
I'm grounded in you My Creator and in you I can appreciate the newness in learning.
Living in your presence. Learning in your presence.

I hope for an answer to my prayer.
What is clear is your love, your hand in my life, and your wisdom.

Completing this life and this dream with joy is my learning.
So, I'm learning to live again and I'm learning to dream again.
Dreaming to learn, dreaming to live.
Learning.

Stand

Sometimes gravity weighs heavy on me like a dead corpse.
As I stand—I feel as if I'm falling to the ground.
This heavy tightness in my chest.

As I am standing—I want to do what's right.
As you were falling, I watched you fall and did nothing.
I want to stand up against injustice. I want to stand for justice.

This world desires to choke life out of me.
Honestly sometimes I cower in presence of adversity and opposition.
When I should stand—sometimes I fall and falter.

Why don't I stand up for myself?
Why don't I stand up for what is right?
Why don't WE stand up for what is right?

When will we stand up and take our rightful positions?
Why don't I, why don't we stand up to opposition?
Why don't I, why don't we fight for what we know is right.

I need to stand.
We need to stand.
Stand with me.

Poetry

Part One

Poetry you wrap me in your arms.
Poetry you make me smile.
Like literally invigorate me.
With alliterations, similes, poetry you make me your metaphor.
Poetry, metaphorically you make me a new person when you're near me.

Poetry you make all the imperfect parts of me whole.
You make the noun, "I am", the verb "I am."
And figuratively speaking you make me there and here all at the same time.
Poetry you defy time.
The way you plant me in the most sumptuous scenarios.

Poetry your moves melt me.
Poetry you pull me into new dimensions, and you push me into new galaxies.
Poetry you remember me.
You remember my birthday.
And you surprise me with new birthday rhymes, I love our birthday lines.

You remember my last laugh.
Poetry you bring me joy on a sad day.
You turn me up, when I want to be down.
Poetry you inspire me.
Poetry you are my love.

Poetry you keep me smiling,
Like, ha, ha, ha, ha, ha, ha, ha.
Poetry you riddle me pink.
Poetry you are the fragrance at the brim of my nose.
Poetry you are the vase to my rose.

Poetry, you are the ink to my paper.
Poetry,
Poetry be the words to my life.
Oh Poetry, Oh Poetry, inspire me.
Oh Poetry, Oh Poetry, you inspire me.

BLUE

If I were blue,
I would be royal.
So, I would see me for who I am.

If I were blue,
I would be the blue of the sea.
Deeper than eyes can see.

If I were blue, I would be the blue of the sky.
All the beautiful hues of blues in the earth would be me.
If I were blue, I wouldn't be melancholy.

I would be a brilliant blue.
I would contemplate the creator's glorious splendor in a blue serenity.
My blue would reflect the God in me.

If I were blue, the lush green meadows would melt into me.
Making a soft serene seafoam blue-green.
Covered by light blue hues, this is my blue.

Looking for space

Looking for space to find out who I am.
Looking for space to believe.
Looking for space to enjoy each day.
Looking for space in my life—for me.

Looking for space in my mind.
Looking for space.
Looking for space.
Looking for peace.

Looking for space, sometimes I want to run away.
Looking for space so I can find me.
Looking for space, I need space.
Looking for space, space to grow.

Looking for space, I need peace.
Looking for space thinking "I just want to be alive."
Looking for space.
Looking for peace.

Looking for space in my heart.
Looking for space in my mind.
Looking for space to love.
Looking for space to learn to walk.

Looking,
Looking.
Looking for space.
Looking for peace.

Fantasy Island

There's a place I go when I want to fade away.
A place not too far from fantasy, and not too far from the authentic truth.

In this place, I can swim through the sky.
I can float against waves as they hit the sandy beach where land and ocean meet.

I can blend with the kaleidoscope colors of sand.
I can recess my body against the clouds as they are support me.

I sashay through the sky, and I just melt into the wind.
To escape the commonplace of myself, I go to the world within my mind.

Imagination, creation,
ingenuity, this is my being.

Here away on this island I start to form new landscapes.
New places to fly to.

I live the life where death is not possible,
and only life, newness, and fresh ideas are possible.

Sometimes I want to live here in this place forever,
But I know that it's an abstract aberration of actuality.

An intricate imaginary imprint of a vision that's make-believe.
Drawn up dreams, dancing delicately on this fantasy island.

Fortune Cookies

Reading: "You're coming into you own power enjoy! **Numbers:** 1,2,3,4,5,6,7,10,12"

Yeah right—if gaining power was as easy as cracking open fortune cookies.

Well I would be buying more Chinese food.

Even though fortune cookies weren't invented in China,

But were invented California—small detail.

Yes, this fortune has got to be true!

Oh Wait, IT IS!

This fortune cookie may be on to something.

Fortune cookies that are filled with know it all comments.

Are bound to be right in an instance.

After all, I am coming into my own power.

ORANGE, GREEN, VIOLET

Red, Yellow, Blue

What makes us, is you.

Yet you hardly ever want to mix with us.

I mean what's wrong with us?

You made us, yet you hardly ever want to be seen with us.

You loved us, and now we're just bi-products of who you use to be.

You, you, you,

You used to love being here.

You, you, you,

You used to want to be near.

And we didn't have to persuade you.

We didn't have to bat our eyes for you to see us.

Or think to bribe you for you to give us the time of day.

You would luxuriate over our stunning hues.

And we cossetted you, you and your handsome hues.

Oh, how we would relish in each other hands blending and mixing together.

We used to play all night in the same space, under the same sky, swept away in the same grace.

And now we don't even speak.

What happened to us?

Are we truly no longer adequate for you?

Answer me Red.

Blue you hear me I know you do, and you yellow—hello?

We are here, knocking on your door,

What makes us, is you.

Artist

Halima "Artist" Brown

Apple of God's eye, I was created.

Apple in my hand--running home, saying "Mom, I made this."

Artist, middle name started with an "A" so to me it was the same thing.

I only saw myself as the canvas.

I am the pencil, the pen, the paintbrush, the marker, and the oil pastels.

I've started to see that I am the canvas colored saturated with images.

My dreams come alive with each movement of my hand.

Weaving the life of each image into existence, I create.

I am the creator of my creations.

I am, as I make, as I watch, art unfold.

I'm the image of the one who made me.

I create like my Heavenly Father.

Not planets or universes, nor people or animals.

I create a different kind of art.

Art from the sea, art from trees, art from the sky.

Arts from depictions, art from abstract ideas and bold beautiful imageries.

I am God's creative artistic daughter.

Art is what I do.

An Artist is who I am creatively.

Daughter of the Creator is who I am.

Tonight

The day proved to be successful.
The hours favored all you had planned.
Tonight, the stars shine bright and light up your world.

Tonight, you've made it.
Made it through another day.
Made it to the finish line, tonight.

Enjoy the view and the sweet scent of your work tonight.
Tonight, is Yours. Yes, tonight is Mine.
Tonight, is Ours.

Better

I hunger for this,

this opportunity to be better.

To think better, to walk better, to live better.

To illustrate better, to paint better, to express myself better.

To dance better, move better, groove to the music of life—better.

To breathe better.

To just be = Better.

Better is not a dream I cannot live,

it is a moment that each day gives.

I must learn to live each day better.

Better for me, and no one else.

Better for me, time to live for self.

Better for me, so I can see that I am the better I need.

I've always needed me

to see me better.

Better for the mother inside of me.

Better to the Sister that I want to be.

Better to the growing parts of me.

Better to the broken parts of me.

Better to the inside of me that I see, but I allow few to see.

Better—Because I don't want to be hurt by anyone anymore.

So, I hide me, because it's taken years to get BETTER.

Better to protect me,

from the you of the past.

Better for the new me.

Am I the better me that I believed I can be?

What have I been waiting on?

I see BETTER staring back at me.

Better for the hope of today.

Better for tomorrow a hope not that far away.

Better for the times I'll need more from myself.

And I'll possess everything inside of me to produce—Better.

Better for the me inside of me.

Better for the woman I am, and the woman I am going to be.

Better for the me I am, and the me I am going to be.

Better.

Prayers

I look to you.

I look to you, just as I did as a child.

When I wanted to run away from all my troubles.

When my hope, felt hopeless.

I look to you.

I pray to you YHWH, my Heavenly Father, my Daddy, my Creator, my Abba

I am inside the care of my Lord, my Savior, my Redeemer, my Big Brother,

And the Lover of my heart.

I pray, and I pray, and I pray.

I pray, a prayer, and say Amen.

Then I wait, and do it all over again.

I believe in you Lord.

I know that you are the truth.

When my tears are like wells springing from my eyes.

When my hope is dim, and I'm holding on for dear life.

Whether loud, silent, screaming, or speaking.

Knelling, sitting, laying in my bed or standing,

Hear my prayers.

Chapter 4 Breakdown

Chapter Four: Create your way out

In this chapter my determination was to explore my creativity as a recovery method. With the idea of how can, I use my gifts to heal my heart, mind, and soul. This was artistic and emotional road to recovery, and I needed it.

Writing

I've been writing since I was seven years old, and I love it. This poem exudes my joy and passion for writing.

Art

This poem is about the beautiful and positive ethos that is art. Art is so powerful means of self-expression.

Through you

A poem about movement, and the power of using it to travel through your personal space and through the universe.

Learning

In life we learn in so interesting ways there's experience, learned behavior, world and social norms, family, friends, school and schools of thought. Learning is adventurous and scary all at the same time.

Stand

This poem is a call for justice, strength, unity, movement, and conversation of the complexity that is a relationship outside our immediate selves and community.

Poetry: Part One

A conversation with poetry, I how it makes my love flow to it.

Blue

It is transformed into so much more than my favorite color, I use it to connect to world. I hope you enjoy this sweet poem.

Looking for space

At first thought I wanted to cry at the meaning of this poem, then the second thought comes, and I laugh out load. To explain, living a life as someone who was sexual abused, physical abused, domestic abused, or has experienced form of abuse, assault, injury, and grief, space is more important than one may think initially. Initially someone may think smother the person with all the love in the world. Or maybe the thought of a loved one is leave them alone, they need to sort it out themselves. Space may seem like something to exists without effort, but on the contrary the right amount of space can make or break a person. This poem is about finding the right amount of space for me.

Fantasy Island

This poem is about creating something new out of a thought, like poetry does.

Fortune Cookies

True story, I ate some pretty good Chinese-American food from a local restaurant and I received this fortune. Oh, I was so mad at that little piece of paper. It took me over a year to write this short poem, mainly because I had to let go of my frustration connected to why I thought, I wasn't "walking into my own power."

ORANGE, GREEN, VIOLET: Red, Yellow, Blue

I think this one poem is clear, but just in case it's wasn't here's one word "origin".

Artist: "Halima Artist Brown"

So, I started to call myself "Halima Artist Brown," around 7 or 8 years old. I thought I should give myself a new name, which ironically was just as unbelievable as my actual middle name. I would later have to explain if questioned, but I thought it made since at the time.

Tonight

This poem is about being in the moment. In the very moment you are in now, and then excepting it for what it.

Better

"Better" is a poem about wanting more out of life. It's about staying hungry for growth, development, and love. At some point, I thought it's got to be more than that, it's got to truly be about me. It's not just the results that come from me, but the patience, the passion, kindness, joy and love that flows through me and to me. That is the ultimate better and is the better I now want and aspire to.

Prayers

His poem is about the prayer process between me and the Creator, The Architect of my life. In life our prayers increase and decrease with the ups and downs of life. I think it is necessary to be intentional about keeping a prayer life as an adolescent or adult.

Chapter 5

Sacred

Altar

My heart needs you.

It bleeds, blood for you.

My heart cry's, it cry's tears for you.

Longing for the love that only you can give me.

Longing for your voice to speak.

Lord, speak to me.

Listening on bended knees.

In the middle of the prayer, thinking— "My heart needs you"

I'm crying Lord do you hear me?

This alter I have built for you.

I'm here visit me.

This alter is here for you Lord.

I am here at this altar crying— "Lord I need you."

I bring to you the worst of me,

An offer to you to exchange the old me for the new me in you.

This is me, my body, a living sacrifice. I hope it is pleasing to you.

Lord do you see me?

I'm here at the altar of my heart.

The Strength of a Woman

The strength of woman is not found in her curves.
It's found in her powerful boldness, strength, and passion.
It's found in her patient, loving, and kind words.
It's found behind her thoughts, not her behind.

Listen to her thoughts and you can hear,
see, feel and imagine
what is in her heart.
and mind.

It's not written on her lips.
It doesn't drip off her mouth like water from a melon.
But it flows out of her as beautiful rays that break through the clouds.
Like morning sun flows from the sky like a beautiful waterfall.

Her powerful words cascade across her tongue
and over her lightly painted lips.
They collide with your eardrums.
Her words tell you "your perfectly imperfect, and your power inside you is LOVE."

A strong woman has the DNA inside of her to create life.
Every travailing labor pain in her life was worth it.
The power of woman is given to her at birth—it is given to her in the heavens.
Planted in her heart and in her mind and as she lives it shines.

The strength of a woman is her desire to express herself,
Through speech, dance, song, rhyme, reason or color.
Her desire to please her makers,
"Mommie daddy look—look what I made."

It's her as child wanting to dress like her mother, or her favorite heroine.
Trying on heels or fixing her father's tie before work.
It's her singing your favorite songs
to cheer you up, over and over until it works (made you smile).

Her love, her heart, her passion,
the ways she cares.
From child to young woman,
she'll grow-up to be a beautiful, sophisticated, strong woman.

The power of a woman comes from within her.
And from the people who water her spirit with love and compassion.
When the sun shines on her spirit like love, she grows in all the right directions.
Love, joy and peace motivates her to greatness, because she was born with purpose.

The strength of a woman is not found in her hair.
But in the length and depths of her heart is how you'll know her.
The strength of a woman sometimes compared to Jewels.
It can be summed up by one word "Amen."

The strength of a woman is a voyage designed by the narrow roads she walks.
The path of righteousness she leaves behind her, by peaceful talks.
Her actions may seem meek and mild, and powerless, but humility is her crown.
For with loving words woman she can end a war and heal hearts.

Her strength and power enlighten.
The strength of a woman is to use her wisdom, her power, her love.
She must recognize her weaknesses are strengths too.
She stands in the face of adversity as women always do and conquer it.

Love Me **More**

Lord I long for your touch.
But I am in the arms of someone who could never love me like you do.
Lord I yearn for your love, but I continue to knock at another's door.
Lord it's taken me years to see that no one can love me more.

Lord you brought my life, with your life.
Lord you gave your body for mine.
Lord I need you to show me my value.
Lord I need you to show my worth.

Show me why you died for me?
Lord show me why you think about me, have plans for, why you birthed me?
Lord show me why you carried me in my mother's womb?
Lord show me why I matter to you?

Lord show me, so I can look to you.
Lord show me, so that I can pursue you.
I need to know why you look at me?
Why do you look at me at all?

Why do you gaze down from your throne to see me?
Why do you smile when you see me?
With all my failed attempts to do good.
With all my failed attempts to do anything at all.

Why hope for me?
What is it about me that you love so much?
Why do you love me so much that you won't let me go?
You give me free will to choose if I will be ensconced in my erroneous ways.

You refuse to see me give up.
You refuse to let me fail.
Each day you give me new tools, you show me that you are my hummer and nail.
Each day You teach me how to live, so now my life to you I give.

Lord,
I need You.
Lord I need you in my life.
I need you in my heart, my mind, my soul.

Lord I need your love more.
Lord I need to love you more.
Lord I need you more.
Lord love me more.

PACE GIRL

Part One

Pace,
Pace,
Pace.

Sometimes, I pace back and forward.
Sometimes I walk in circles.
Sometimes I walk, and walk, and walk.
Then I stop and see that I've gotten nowhere.
All I've done is draw a circle in the sand.

Pacing back and forth,
Looking for the most pleasurable path, conversant with instant gratification.
Pacing side to side, looking for comfort, but finding none.
Pacing, pacing, looking for a path.
And habitually choosing the wrong one.

Pacing,
Pacing.
Pacing.

When will I stop moving?
Stop rushing, stop moving before life's guiding light goes on.
I want to pace myself, I want to breathe, and I want to grow.
I need to pace myself, I need to breathe, and I need to grow.
Like the lily in my planted flower pot.

I want to grow like the seed planted in good soil—I want to grow too.
I want to stretch my limbs out to the glow of the sun too.
To feel the light to kiss my limbs,
as they stretch open at day break.
To feel the light, move through the blades of my leaves.

Pace Girl,
Pace Girl,
Pace Girl—to grow.

I want to be watered when it rains.
When He reigns.
But I've got to pace myself.
Pace myself.

Pace Girl.

Sometimes I think I don't have what it takes to succeed.
Don't have what it takes to reach a goal.
Don't have what it takes to meet the mark.
Don't have what it takes to make it.
Don't have what it takes to own who I am and to stand in my own shoes.

To live my dream. To dream a dream. To live my life.
But Inside I know I do I have what it takes.
I have what it takes to do it all—as I pace myself.

I have what it takes to be who I was called, created, shaped and fashioned to be.
I have what it takes to be who I am.
I must pace.
Finally, I stop.
Take a step back for a change.

I switched it up.
Now everything has changed.
I changed my pace, and my direction.
In my shoes, I am walking.
In my dreams, I am dreaming.

I'm pacing.
I'm pacing.
I'm pacing.

Faster, I'm walking this time.
But I'm in sync.
I'm matching up to my life now.
I have found my feet permanently.
I am, who I am meant to be.

Then I think.
Just, PACE GIRL.
Pace.
Pace.
Pace.

TEMPLE

God created the temple to dwell with his people on earth. Inside of the Temple are special items. Some are used for worship, others for praise. They are all symbols of God's love for Us, His people, His children.

Secret places.
If only this war that I feel raging inside me would end.
I wonder should I give my worries to you?
Will you help me get through this?
Will your perfect will have its way?
Inside and outside?

Inside and outside.
People see, but they have no idea what is built inside of me.
My bones that had to be broken,
My heart could expand enough to love you.
My spine that had to be adjusted,
I can stand straight in your presence.

The eye's that had to be reopened after years of callus, and blindness.
How my ears had to be pierced by your gentle words.
Words strong enough to open them up.
I know that this war inside of me will end — so I can have peace.
I know you have given me all the things I need, inside of me.
To conquer this thing and anything else.

I conquer everything with you, in you.
I can defend myself from this internal war that rages.
I was born to be different, a culture changer, a force not easily shaken.
What's inside of me was put there for a reason.
What's inside of me will be used, in its due season.
Inside my Temple, is a Spirit that is Holy.

Every moment of grace.
Every place of praise.
Every place of worship was built for me.
I was destined for this position, mission, and secret dwelling place.
My temple has corners filled with love.
Open spaces covered with your joy and peace.

A table to place all my worries on.
A mercy seat that resembles the one in heaven.
A sun room that bursts with effulgent energy.
A quite place to mediate on God's words during life.
A music room where I can play instruments and left up praises.
As place to be brought to perfection, through brokenness and being lost.

A place to learn to regain hope.
After years of looking through shattered glass and broken windows,
And bruised walls, and red eyes.
People see me, and they have no idea what is on the inside.
My temple is my home.

Here I am closer.
Here I am free.
Here I am loved.
My temple, my home, my secret place.
Dwell within me — Elohim.
Stay here with me — in My Temple.

Credence

There is a place inside my heart,
Where there are pieces of my brokenness.
The table on which I place my entire being.
Here I am, an offering to you YHWH, broken but yours.

Please know that you mean everything to me.
Please know you always have.
Now I want to show you.
Now I want to place at your feet—all of me.

I want you to see me.
Places that are ugly, battered, tired, beautiful, sensitive, blessed, intolerable parts of me.
This heart I have inside my chest belongs to you—only you.
Heavenly Father do you see, Abba Daddy do you see your daughter—it's me.

I am yours.
YHWH your perfect love produced me—you made me.
You are my Creator, my Lord, my God, my Father, my Daddy, my Love.
I hope that you can see this—this open heart her on this table.

Searching for Me

I search for me in your Genesis,
Hoping to find some obvious Revelation.
I search for me in your eyes.
Light brown completion of the earth you created me form.

Molded me from it, and I am, the image of you.
I see this earth, that you placed me in.
In your words, I look for my existence.
For my internal origins.

My organs are bleeding to know the me, that you know completely.
Me, the tree that bares good fruit.
All I want is to be the person you see.
A lover of truth, truth seeker who desires to live in your wisdom and in grace.

Like someone who bares love.
Like someone who wears love, like the feathers that adorn the peacock.
Not someone lays bodies on the ground, nor covets with an envious eye.
Not someone who spreads hurtful deceptions or falsehoods.

But someone who wears hoods—hoods that cover the eyes of an innocent son.
Hoods that protect without taking lives.
Hoods that birth great poets.
Great Artists, Dancers, Singers, Musicians, great Lyricist—whose lyrics HIT.

Like these lyric HIT.
HITS all the right places to heal, give, and console.
Lord your lyrics touch my heart, just like your love bleed for my soul.
This poem is to tell you—I love you.

Search me Lord and know me.
Search me Lord and find me worthy.
I affectionately desire your love. Search me Lord and see a heart for you.
Search for me Lord, and I hope when you find me I'm here loving you.

Blood

We all watched as the blood trickled out of their once dynamic body.
Dripping onto the earth, splattered across the ground as your body was put down.
Your brothers, my brothers, our brothers are dying, laying dead—cold blood.
Your sisters, my sisters, our sisters are lying face down, laying dead—cold blood.
Dead from someone's interpretation of justice, hate or an evil plan for revenge.

Some people think that taking someone life is free.
Free like a life of the pursuit of liberty, life, and happiness.
They say that you don't deserve it—Life. They are cold blooded.
So, they walk around and take it—Life.
Cold blooded murders, abusers, liars, stealers of life.

Or does their hatred towards others consume them with malice, lies and destruction?
Do they ever use wisdom and walk through shame, frustration, regret, guilt, or hurt?
Do they use hate to walk through life as taker?
Abusing their rights as authority, as civilians, by constantly taking innocent life?
Do you lend your ears to a lie, or are you a victim of someone who acted on a lie?

Now your son, your husband, your brothers, our uncles, and your nephews are dead.
Now our sons, our husbands, our brothers, our uncles, and our nephews are dead.
Now your daughter, your wife, your sisters, our aunts, and your nieces are dead.
Now our daughters, our wives, our sisters, our aunts, and our nieces are dead.
Senseless killings, senseless blood.

Are you a killer—Blood thirsty man?
Did you kill me with your hate—Blood thirsty men?
Or did I let my anger kill you—Blood?
Secretly you take life, and then lie and hid it.
Secret lives of hate—Blood?

They take life then want to be spared.
Hung you, but didn't want to be hung?
Anger—blood red.
I'm angry at the ways of this wicked, unjust twisted life—blood red.
Rage, hurt, exploitation is killings and taking lives.

Intentionally peeling open a world of hate.
Hate that kills.
Hurt that kills.
Hurt that bleeds blood.

Bleeding, Blood, people killings and taking lives.

Now your looking down at the ground.
Now your hands are soiled with blood.
But you weren't the one that killed him.
But you witnessed it and said nothing, what does that make you?
What if you just watched as the blood pour out of his open heart?

Cold grey concrete, dark warm red on dark grey concrete.
A voice, calling to you, call for help, I'm still alive, if you could just call for help.
No one called, no-one came to her aid. She died.
What if you just watched as the blood pour out of her open heart?
Could love we have our sister more—is love watching her dying?

What if you saw it, but said you didn't?
What if you lied? Does that make you a killer?
Does a lack of action make you at fault?
By default, are their blood on our hands too?
What if I just watched –Am I an accomplice to murder?

Can murder cleanse the blood from hands—killer?
Blaming others for the things you do, when this murder is your doing?
Is this blood on your shirt going to come out?
Can anyone tell that you are a murder?
Can anyone tell that you just took a life—DOES murder show?

Barely breathing,
holding unto my breath,
counting them as they left my body.
Coughing blood.
Blood filling my lungs, I'm not sure if I'm going to make it.

Dying.
Bleeding blood.
All this bloodshed,
And still pools of blood seems commonplace.
Blood.

Does murder show, like love shows?
Does it glow, or does it dim your light?
How much of this was caught on camera?
Are there cameras here?
Are there cameras here?

Is there someone hiding behind that bush?
Is this bush burning?

Or is your conscience burning to say— "I did it?"
I did it—I killed my brother, I killed my sister.
The stain did come out your robes, but the stains didn't fade from your heart.

No, it stained your mind, now it's gesticulating to the outside world.
But you keep it silent, you've justified your wrongs.
And washed your hands with lies.
Blood lust stains in your vain—like a killer with a blood crave.
BLEEDING—BLOOD.

I know that it wasn't as if you hated your brother.
Cain, I look at you sometimes, and I think "Why?"
Then I think I know your hurt.
What would I have done?
Blood. Bleeding. Blood. Dying.

It's not easy to be wrong—murder with a conscious.
But it's not right to be wrong—killers who don't care.
What have you done—Blood? What have we done—Blood?
What have we done—Cous? What have we done shedding all this—Blood?
Blood what how you done?

You justified raping a child, and you do it again.
You justified taking her innocence, as she bleeds inside.
Inside she is dying, and you are smirking wickedly with your delusions.
Young girls and boys losing their childhood, because of grown man and woman.
OUR CHILDREN ARE BLEEDING—BLOOD.

Blood abuse, blood abuses.
Using their authority, and power for detestable actions and venomous depravity?
Weak people like to see children bleed—our children are bleeding, blood.
Children abusing children, because of what evil adults taught them.
Child abusing, sexual abusing children, mental and emotional abusing children.

Can I forgive my enemy? After he raped me?
After my first boyfriend raped me, wanted to marry me, then attempted to kill me?
After another helped me kill my first child?
After he uses my painful past and bad decisions against me?
Yes, I can forgive them all. Bleeding heart and all.

Can we forgive my enemy?
After they killed our brother and our sister,
Could we love an enemy or forgive them?
Could a slave forgive their slave master?
I hate you, I hate you, but can I forgive you?

Am I pray my enemies? Are we able to pray for our enemies? Damn.
Or would I want blood? Or would I see blood? Man, this is hard.
Am I willing to take your life, and lose my life—bloods?
Am I willing to take your life, and lose my life—Crips?
Blood. Bleeding. Blood. Dying.

The streaks of blood falling down my eyes as I cry out for my own life.
Red in my anger for my enemies' blood.
Blood.
Retaliation is blood stained sidewalks, white chalk, and lost loves.
As I watch me, as I watch me dying, left cheek of the sidewalk.

Everyday people, telling others they don't matter.
Mad at one another because of what someone said or may have said.
Blood—is the madness in our mind.
Blood—is the clarity of what is in our sound mind.
Blood—Must my death be the only thing that speaks?

Do we care? Yes, we care. We have always cared for our brothers and sisters.
Yes, we have always cared for each other. Your life matters. Yes, so does mine.
Yes, our blood is our common ground, and innocent lives should not be gunned down.
And another burial shouldn't say more than what we say to each other, face to face.
Yes, we care and it's time to show it by not shedding blood.

Love—Bleeds Blood.
Love—Bleeds Blood.
Love—bleeds Red.
Love—Bleeds Red Blood.
Blood in a heart—Red. Bloodred.

A Praying Mother

All the years without you.
All those years alone.
I always remember you saying on our phone calls, "pray."
When something goes wrong—pray.
When all else failed, when I'd call you crying—You say "Pray."
I knew you were praying for me.
I knew all those my nights alone you were praying.
Were nights you spent on your knees pleading to God on my behalf.
A praying mother I that didn't truly know.
Still I knew you were a thousand miles away always praying for me.
I wonder how many times our prayers reached God's ear simultaneously?
As we live and breathe can we pray for a change in our hearts towards each other?
Or is this just a daughters' prayer?
Today, I thank God that I have a praying Mother.

Black Lives Matter

Black lives matter, not because of the skin.
But because the person is a person.
Not because of a march, because of the life, that is recognized by the march.
Because of the lives that were lost.

Because Cain should have never killed Able.
Because brothers should look out for each other.
Because we should care about more than ourselves.
Because when one suffers, we all suffer.

But so many fail to see that.
But they see the color of my skin as weapon that makes me dangerous.
My skin, my worth, my strength, my heart, and intelligence are mine.
Mine.

Mine to have.
Not yours to fear.
Mine to live for.
Not yours to kill.

Mine to teach my children, and my family.
Not yours to steal with your bigotry, brutality, bitterness.
My life to share in prosperity and my life to gain prosperity.
Not yours to hinder with schemes of sacrilege and scarcity.

Stop.
I did.
Freeze.
I'm frozen.

Hands up.
They are as high as the sky,
Yet seconds later, I lose my breath.
I'm gone – Dead.

Dead, gasping for their last breaths as they abscond from their body.
With your hateful hands around my neck, strangling me,
As you're screaming that I was resisting arrest.
Black life DEAD.

Dead, leaving school to go home.
Dead, walking on the sidewalk.
Dead, because I took my hands out of my pocket to put them where you could see.
Dead – only for you to call a pen in hand, a gun.

Dead, because they wanted to walk to a corner store.
Dead, because you think black people shouldn't live anymore.
Dead, with a bullet in their head.
Dead with your hatred ripping through my chest like a hot bullet from a trigger.

Your hate for yourself, reflects outwardly to you killing – Black lives.
Dying, losing – Black lives.
Gone until eternity – Black lives.

There's no reason to shove this matter under the rug any longer.
As it has been done for years and years, and hundreds of years before.
So, this time we're talking.
This time we're saying, we can't take watching you take black lives anymore.

America.
America.
America.
America.

We are living — Black lives.
We are given — Black lives.
We are growing up — Black lives.
We are fruitful — BLACK LIVES.

We matter to us.
We matter to us.
We are matter.
We are here too.

We don't fear you.
We don't run from fear.
We eradicate it.
WE ARE BLACK LIVES MATTER.

We are standing up.
We are standing up.
We are standing up,
FOR BLACK LIVES MATTER — TO US.

Water

Your love covers me,
It washes me with your grace.
I know you have given your life for me.
That you are my living water.
You are my well that never runs dry.
The spring that overflows.
The ocean deep you created it.
All that flows from heaven comes from you.
You are good, and your goodness abounds and flows here on earth.
Waters of the heaven above, release to the earth below.
When it rains in heaven, let it rain on earth.
Loose the blessings of the living water in heaven.
Flow living water here on earth.
Water, you have always supplied abundantly for all my needs.
Water, you have always been the overflow to the dry parts of me.
Water run throw the valleys of my life.
Water flow to the hills of my belief.
Water be all that we need.
Water cover the attacks from the enemy that try to rise up against us.
Water cover our apprehensions, faithlessness, and fears.
Water spring forth from our heart with hope.
Water lift our faith beyond our imagination.
Cradle us over the ocean as we walk with you on water.

Chapter 5 Breakdown

Chapter Five: Sacred

Sacred is about what my relationship with YHWH, my love, and my heart toward Him. It's also about issues, important matters that I care about. This was such an enjoyable chapter to write, for those who know me personally, I love me some Hosanna/ Jesus/Yeshua/Christo. It was also challenging to write because, it was personal and vulnerable different from pervious chapters.

Altar

This poem is about where I want my heart to be. Ideally, it's positioned in the direction of God.

The Strength of a woman

Unfortunately, I didn't grow up around strong women. When writing this poem, I had to reach into a place that didn't innately exist. I also learned that I am strong, and I do come from a lineage of strong women.

Love me more

This poem is about knowing that no matter it is, myself included, no-one can or will love me like God. It's like a memo to myself and a plea to God at the same time.

Pace Girl: Part One

One of my favorite poems I've ever written, this poem was inspired by the Non-Profit Organization" Pace Center For Girls." It is a center that works with at risk girls, by educating and preparing them to be great leaders, thinkers, and great contributors in their lives and their communities. I wanted this poem to provoke thoughts in the mind of these girls and challenge these girls to think about the direction the are moving in their lives. It's such an honor to write and this poem. I hope to inspire these amazing young girls and young women.

Temple

"Temple" is poem about meeting God in a place of worship and praise. There's the idea that our body is the temple, so I communicate with apprehensions and my faith to my Creator in that place.

Credence

This poem is about laying all of me at the feet of my Creator.

Searching For Me

Poetically and spiritually I wanted to expound of a thought I had one day; which was "I God looked down at me, what would I be doing?"

Blood

The poem Blood was written to address, senseless killing of children, youth, women and men, murders, child sexual abuse, homicides, and violence in communities.

A Praying Mother

This poem is about the distance between my Mother and I during my lifetime. It's also about the closeness we have as believers, a gift I received from my Moher.

Black Lives Matter

A poems topic is current, but more than current it's personal and heart felt. Black lives have always mattered to the Black, Brown, African, and Africans in American community. This poem explores the gruesome facets of potential whys black lives are being gunned down, attacked, and devalued? I decided to make it as visual as possible, poetically and emotionally.

Water

The inspiration for this poem was the restorative and transformative power of water. As-well-as the idea of who is my Savior to me, and how do I interact within that relationship.

Chapter Six

Greater Than

Greater Than

Dear Self,

Please know that you are one of the Creators exceptional creations. You are the Heavenly Father's very good and GREATER than work on this earth. You are GREATER Than anything this world has said about you. You are GREATER than the things of this world, because of He who lives in you is GREATER. Be yourself. Be authentically awesome. Be brave and be bold. Be you. Be GREATER THAN. GREATER than you've ever imagined, and then imagine again. Keep living for GREATER THAN.

Love,

Yourself

Jamaica

Warmth and curiosity, bellows as the wind sweeps across your face,
Then the scent of fresh flowers, sea salt and sand.
Hot—cold water rescues you from the rays of the sun,
You plant yourself in an aqua blue sea.

Cool—this morning we climbed the tree and after school is let out.
We will enjoy a fresh coconut water under the shade of a palm tree.
Swimming in the ocean.
Swinging on the limbs of your favorite tree.

Jumping into water, as you dive into the nearest waterfall.
Crashing into waves, as you run from land to the ocean.
You slowly stroll into town ready for the meal you know awaits you.
Mother's cooking is the best, or someone with the secrets of recipes once unread.

The sunset meets your eyes at the days horizon,
As you take a bite of roasted bread fruit—Yes.
Yes, someone here loves you.
Jamaica—This is where I started.

This is where my story began.
I am a seed planted,
uprooted sooner than I could have ever planned.
Left my Motherland and moved to a foreign land.

Jamaica, you raised me.
Jamaica, you gave me the best parts of my life.
Jamaica all of our beautiful memories.
Jamaica, I miss you.

Jamaica, I miss your streets and marketplace.
Miss your fountains, your waterfalls, your rivers and streams.
You're my air and you're my song, my Jamaica.
Jamaica, each day your song carried me, carried me, carried me on.

Daughter

If I could protect you from everything that could harm you,
So that nothing would ever hurt you—I would.
If I could show you that there's no monsters under your bed.
That there's nothing in your closet that worth hiding from.
If I could make all the bad things disappear—I would.

If you needed me, and I was thousands of miles away.
I would fly to you as fast as I could, to be there, here, by your side.
If you needed a hug or a band- aid on your tiny knee scrape.
Or you needed me to change your frown around, I would be there.
I would hold you and hug you and show you that I love you.

If I could always be on the other end of the phone,
When you needed to tell me about a new discovery.
If you stood on top of the highest point in the world,
I wouldn't stop until I reached you.
I would part the Red Sea to get to you—I would for you.

Sweetheart I would answer every call — I would for you.
But I can't be there, because I'm here fighting for you.

I'm here blocking all the arrows from coming in your direction.
I'm here preparing a future for you.
I'm here making sure there are no monsters underneath your bed.
I'm here making sure your present is as bright as your future.
I'm here showing your enemies you are not one to be missed with.

Daughter, I want to slay every fire breathing dragon for you.
Daughter, I won't be able to fight all your battles.
Daughter, one day you will feel pain, and it's really going to hurt.
But you'll have to let yourself see your own strength,
But I know that one day you'll have to go up against them without me.

My Daughter, my Love, you mean so much to me.
Daughter forgive me because I'm not perfect—I wish I could be for you.
Know that you inspire me to be my best.
Know that it's the best of me that makes the best of you.
And I need you to be smart, be brave, be bold, be free.

Daughter, please be as free as possible.
My daughter know that all things are possible.

One word that would express what I feel for you,
One word to explain why you are my joy,
One word would have to be "Love". I love you."
I will always be in your heart, now and forever more.
Daughter, I wish I could make you understand that I would do anything for you.

If I could make you understand that you are the sun in my sky.
That you are the apple in my eye,
That you are the reason why I always smile.
I would wear a "Proudest Parent" T-Shirt every day,
But it would fall apart after a while.

Together, we'll learn that you can do anything that you can imagine and so much more.
We will create a space brimming with butterflies.
A bounteous green meadow with fields of blossoming flowers,
Where we can run freely and smell the saturated aromatic breeze.
There's nothing I wouldn't do for you, and what I can do I will.

Here in our space we would dream, dreams and believe that they could all come true.
You and me together.

I will be all you need me to be.
I will be all you can imagine.
I will be your hero.
I will be your plane.
I will be your lion.
I will be your elephant.
I will be your fish.
I will be your book.
I will be your butterfly.

I will be all these things as we explore this big world together.
I will be there with you the whole way through.

And when I'm not there, remember that I love you.
And when I'm not there, remember that I love you.
And when I'm gone, remember that I love you,
And when I'm gone, remember that I love you
Remember Daughter always that I love you.

LOVE

Love is humble and pure.
Strong and secure.
Love is true and tangible.
Strong and sustainable.
Audacious and affectionate.

Love like arms folded around you.
Love like a kiss from heaven.

Kind and sweet.
Love like the petals of a rose,
Stunning and soft.
Like a peaceful dove descending from heaven.
That is love.

Guidance

Love that last forever.
Hope that carries me through.

Faith that preserves my intellectual fortitude.
Strength that supports my walk into direction and destiny.

Guide me, lead me,
Lord never leave my side.

Who I am, And Who I'm not

Who I am, is who I am.
What I am, is what I am.

I am bold, vivacious and animated,
I am not shy or simple.

I am loving, kind, and sweet.
I am not wicked, I am not cruel, I am not uncouth.

I am patient, tenacious,
passionate and creative.

Who I am, is who I am.
What I am, is what I am.

Flaws

I spent so much time hating me, and my flaws were like battle wounds of self-hate.
I forgot that it wasn't right to wrongfully judge, not even myself.
My mistakes quickly become invisible scars on my body and my face.
How could anything I did erase those flaws

My flaws were wrong discussions.
My flaws were wrong directions.
My flaws were words that shot my heart, like an arrow from a bow.
Flaws telling me to relent, hide, and run.

What is the impact of these hidden scars—flaws?
My flaws don't define me, and my flaws don't tell my complete story—I do.
My flaws are not written all over my face—grace is.
My flaws are not the result of my mistakes—they are a part of my story.

My flaws are not to be teased out or poked at.
My flaws are to be treasured and loved.
My flaws are painted parts of the canvas of my life.
My flaws are not my ending.

My flaws are a part of my beginning.
Beginning of self-love, and self-appreciation.
Beginning of my satisfaction in my life direction and decisions.
My flaws are the wrong roads that lead me back to the truth I once ran from.

The love that I thought I didn't deserve,
I now relish in daily.
My flaws are part of my scars.
My scars are only part of my story.

My flaws are a beauty mark, hidden on my body,
Echoing to the inner me, that I have all you need.
Now it time for me to be.
My flaws are brilliant rays of sun piercing through clouds darkness.

My eyes are now open thanks to my flaws.
My flaws are lifelines pulling me into my new life, telling me it's okay.
Telling me, it's my time.
Telling me—Now begin, now become.

HAPPY

Newly defined for me

You should understand,
I am my own person.
I don't bend or break when you or anyone else says so.

You should understand,
my pretty face doesn't disqualify me from life's pains and hurts,
like people do.

People always think they know me, always think they're right.
That your smile, must be my smile.
Well guess what? —Your wrong.

I don't belong to you, or the thoughts you have of me in your mind.
I am not property of you or your land.
I am a child of God, see that's what defines who I am.

I am who God says I am.
Wonderful, gifted, talented, blessed and highly favored,
above and not beneath.

I am heir to the throne of the Living God, that means I'm royalty.
Blessed in the heaven, because my name is written in the book in heaven.
I'm written in history.

HIStory is my story, but He lived it first.
I can't live it like HE did, but I do my best, to do **ME GREATER**.
I was made in **HIS** image—I look like the Creator.

This is **My** story.
My **MY**stery.
I am written in the word, breathed into existence.

Perfectly, planted in the middle of this garden.
I have dominion, I have power and authority.
Over every animal of the field, the air, and the sea.

I see it now,
I am a powerful being.
Yet I will not boast of this only find joy in my salvation.

Penned into this life, anointed by the oil, oil flowing down my forehead.
Baptized by the Spirit and fire.
I have fire all on me and over me.

I'm learning never abuse the power, always live humble.
I'm learning this is what I am, this is who I am.
What I am is written about me.

The rock that I stand on is strong and is the foundation.
I am a part of the body,
Part of the cornerstone that is used for the building of the Kingdom of God.

The list of who I am makes my mind rattle at times.
How could I be so many things in this one body?
Sometimes I think this can't be me, but it is.

My smile, my mind, my heart, my life,
are made of the substance in which books are written about,
and I'm reading.

So, stop trying to define my happy.
I'm good, I'm Happy, I'm blessed.
My happy is my happy. Defined only by the creator of me.

Good

I am good.
I am good.
I am good because of my Creator.
I am His good thing.

Not by my strength or my deed.
Not by my height or my speed.
I am good, because my Creator made me.
I am good, because my Creator called me.

All good comes from Him.
So, I am—good.
Him who made me,
Makes me good.

Him who saved me, makes me good.
Him who raised me, makes me good.
I am good since I am in the image of good.

Good is never far from me,
I speak to the goodness I want in my life daily.
But by God's spirit, the good spirit in me.

I need His good to produce good.
I need His good to produce goods.
Not by my own merit.

I hope that all that I do has God in it, aspiring to be one with his good Holy Spirit.
I know I must speak into that goodness daily.
His goodness, for His blessing.

Regardless of the pressures that this world puts on me.
Regardless of another's standards, I live will only by your standards.
Regardless of what I may think, I am Good.

I am good because God made me.
When God made me—He said
"This is very good."

Won't look back

Embracing new life,
Letting go of the old.
Walking out of the past, releasing distress, nervousness, and uncertainty.

Holding onto God as my personal GPS.

I walked out of my past thinking, I hope that God is okay with this.
Everything that is, is, what is will fall as it does.
When I look forward I see you Lord, you are in my present and my future.

Assuredly planted in you, my Savior.

You have covered my whole life with your blood.
So, as I leave to this new place I look up to the hills for guidance.
Packing up and forgetting yesterday.

All I want to do is to move forward in God, and to trust God.

I'm not looking back.
Here I am.
I am here—looking forward.

Wrapped

Wrapped up in your rapture.
Overwhelmed by your love and kindness.
Blinded by your glory and grace.
As I daily seek to be in your holy place.

Keep me close to you Lord my God.
Keep me close to you.
Never let me go YHWH.
Never let me go astray.

Help me keep your commandments, to live holy and acceptable to you,
Hold me in the palm of your hand.
Guide me along your path of righteousness.
As narrow as the path maybe—Guide me.

Show me now to separate from this wretched world that keeps calling me.
Keep me from losing hope, as death and sorrow attempt to cloud my vision.
Remind me of the mission of reconciliation and reconcile me to you my first love.
Let me forever be in your presence –my mind stayed on you.

Constantly praying, remaining in my prayer closet, in and out my home.
To seek you first, before your hand, and knowing that you give my heart a home.
Meditating on your word and keeping them in my heart.
Watchfully waiting for your return and keeping my house in order.

Asking for knowledge, wisdom, and understanding.
Lord lead me forever to your side.
Lord let me lay my head upon your chest.
Lord let me kneel before your feet and humble myself before you.

To smile and look up knowing every good thing comes from heaven.
Knowing my life will change as you see fit.
As I learn to have faith while finding joy in it.
Knowing my mind is stayed on you.

Heaven wait for me, as I wait for heaven.
Past-pulls, the future-pushes, as the present holds me,
Reminding me in whose care I dwell in.
Longing to see you in person, to tell you, I love you.

Your heart, your thoughts, your hand and your perfect time.
Wrapped in the abundance of the greatest love of all.
Wrapped up in your love, as I am calmed by the eternal you.
Lord continue to wrap me inside your secret place, Lord I claim you.

I RISE

Like the wind that carries my dreams up to the heavens—I rise.
Like the flames of a fire—I rise.
Like the wings of an eagle—I rise.

I rise
I rise

Like hope—I rise.
Like the words of a prayer—I rise.
On the wings of faith—I rise.

I rise
I rise

Like a phoenix after it transforms from its ashes—I rise.
Like my Savior in a covered tomb—I rise.
Couldn't be held down by death—I rise.

I rise
I rise

With the Lord's mission to redeem and save—I rise.
With the love of God that will never die—I rise.
In His eternal grace—I rise.

I rise.
I rise.

SPRING TIME

As baby buds sprout their heads.
As evergreen trees taunt the leafless trees.
As birds sing and hum.
As children run in fear from buzzing bees.
The frozen winter air turns into a warm gentle breeze.
Patches of yellow grass-finally start to turn green.
It's growing season.
Sweet aromas fill the air.
The perfume of the new season sweeps across a once barren valley.
The ground has awoken,
Spring has sprung.

DON'T WANT TO FALL IN LOVE

I didn't want to meet on that cold winter day.
I didn't want your words to warm all the cold away.
Didn't want your voice to shake my insides.
Didn't want the igloo around my heart to so quickly melt away.

Didn't want to say I love you.
But I love you.
And the thought of you makes me see forever.
Didn't want to say I need you, but I need you.

The thought of you makes me wonder how could I ever live without you?
Didn't want to come out of my shell, because it was warm and cozy in there.
But you pulled me out.
You pulled me out with your sweet gesture, your heart, your words and now I'm here.

Didn't want to be a fall for love.
But I ran into your arms each time you offered them.
Didn't want to say I do,
Instead I said No. No, I'm afraid to jump the broom, but the truth is I didn't want to be hurt again.

Didn't want to be wronged again, to trust again.
I didn't want to open again.
Didn't want to let you in my door again.
I didn't want to hold you close again, because you speak to a part of my soul I didn't know existed.

Didn't want to love again, but your light to shined on me.
You wouldn't let me go, and you stayed as close as to me as I'd let you.
Didn't want you to change me,
But your love for me rearranged me.

It's difficult not to love you when you're waiting at my door like sunshine at daybreak.
I didn't want to love you,
But all I could hear were your gentle, gracious, genuine words that covered my heart like a blanket.
I cannot be cold with you, when I'm with you all I hear are whispers of forever.

Didn't want to care, but you loved me first.
Tried to hide in my shell forever,
but I had to come out and trust—I trust you.
Didn't want to love, but I love you.

Organic

Natural
Effortless
Things just start to fall into place.
Wondering,
What's happening?

Yet knowing it's authentic.
Still having reservations, should I continue?
Thinking, is this organic?
What if I just add Holy water?
Ha, ha, ha not exactly.

This is organic.
He is, I am, yes, we are both perfectly unperfect.
Yet whole and complete.
We're perfect together.
Nothing added that wasn't needed.

Holy Spirit, not holy water—Ha, ha.
You and I have all the right elements.
You match me, and I match you.
Leaving riddles out completely.
Finally—This is right! This is organic.

DEAR ME (_____)

Dear Me,

I love you. You deserved and should have gotten this letter a long time ago. I want you to know that I've loved you from the very beginning of you. Please understand that nothing you have not done in your life makes you less deserving of my love. Please understand that life happened, that you were a child, and you had no firm family structure. So, at times it seemed you were alone. Looking back now, you realize you weren't alone. Life gave you the impression that no-one loved you, but you were always loved by God.

As an adult, mistakes happened, but they do not define you. Nor do your mistakes rule over you. You are not the negativity that sometimes occupies your mind. You are a child of the Living God. You are a strong determined, creative, loving, hard-working, gracious, forgiving person. You've been given a crown, wear it, you are heir to the throne of God. Lift your head up.

Self, you are completely equipped with everything you need to accomplish your dreams. You we were woven together by perfection. You are perfectly you. You are perfectly who you are supposed to be. Be who you are called to be. God has a name for you. God has places for you to go and has destined you to be there. Oh—by the way, your human too, and humans make mistakes. I love you. God loves you. You are loved.

Love,

Yourself

COLORS

I used to see in black and white.

Then I started to see things differently.

See things brighter and more vivid.

I looked at the canvas of my life and colors where everywhere.

I was no longer the words written or the brushstrokes on the paper.

I was the paper filled with

colors.

Girls, Women

As a girl, you learn to color, draw, write and read.
A girl following the women you see, as they watch themselves in the mirror.
As a woman you watch yourself in the mirror.
Wishing you could return to be a girl.

In that moment you remember watching the older women in awe and wonder.

As a girl, you were brave, and you'd leap over puddle larger than you.
In the summer you'd swim further into the lake beyond everyone else.
As a woman you watch the children play at the lake.
You wonder if you would dare to swim again, ever dare to live again?

You realize something has changed.

You have changed, a woman with the weight of the world.
Yet a young reflection of hope still lives in you and will always be there.
You don't need to be a girl, you're a woman.
You don't need to be a woman, you're a girl.

If you are a girl or woman live your power. Exist in who you are.

Morning

Sunshine peaks through a curtain of clouds—whispering "wake up my dear".

Morning dew clings to the windowpanes.

Dew fastens itself to each thin long dark green blade of grass.

A ladybug hugs your finger,

The soft touch of the ladybug reminds you how little it takes to enjoy life.

A bird softly sings its melody.

Carrying your mind to a peaceful place.

The ladybug flies away leaving a small sweet smile on your face.

Clouds part and the glimmering light touches the day,

The sun kisses your forehead,

Beckoning you to explore the day's new adventures,

You sip from your favorite teacup filled with green tea.

You breathe, exhale, and breathe again.

The new day welcomes you in it, enjoy it.

Morning time, a new day has begun.

The Light

The light inside of you will shine in your darkest hour.

When your hope is dim, and you love seems fainter than a dying breath.

The light inside of you will shine through saving you from you.

Sometimes there a temptation to not allow the light to flicker.

Don't be afraid of the light inside of you, instead embrace it.

The light inside of you is faster than the sounds of doubt echoing in your eardrums.

Your light in this universe empowers you to stand up to doubt with faith.

As your light shines the universe shifts.

This light is your life lamp.

Your eyes light are your way makers showing you which path to take as the roads wind.

The light inside of you is great, it is greater than anything else in this world.

This light is the outward reflection of the inward you.

Be the light that shines through.

The world needs the light inside you.

It is beautiful.

Fruits

Love in kind words—breathes in and out patiently as it waits for life to reveal itself.
Joy that echoes a sound of jubilee to the corners of the earth.
Peace that opens doors to a greater life.
Patiently moving through life, hope in my heart, love in eyes, and grace under my feet.
Kindness that gives itself to every circumstance selflessly again, and again.
Mercy upon mercy to keep in a place of constant humility.
Goodness desires more of you than you know you have.
Integrity that makes changes for good and not for flattering or people pleasing.
Faith to know that it will be done, in its season.
Faith to know that every great work that you have done will give you a harvest.
Gentle as a whispered word that heals souls and purifies with the truth.
Truth of what this colorful life is and the knowledge of what this life is not.
Self-control paired with the wisdom and knowledge to flourish during its season.
Ripe with wisdom, knowledge, love, hope, kindness, patience, peace, and gentleness.
The fruits that grow inside of you are the fruits that feed you and keep you alive.

WISDOM

Without judgement

Inquiring insight intently

Searching spirit and soul

Digging deep despite defeats

Onward and optimistic

Moving with purpose

Flowers

Violet, vibrantly, vivaciously commanding attention to your gentle formation.

Lily, unwind and illustrate the precious coloring that line your insides, you don't hide, you surprise.

Sunflowers, brilliant, stature, reaching heights one can only imagine, you stretch your arms and exude delicate strength.

Daisy, life carrier, grasping the rays of light as to expand. Good morning, good day.

Orchid, an array of cultures, poignant, all your bends, lend to your awe.

Rose, as you unfold your story is told, still doesn't capture all that you are. For you protect your secrets with thrones and hues of mystery.

Jasmine, Yasmin as 'A Gift from God.' Divine hope, admiration, fragrant grace, and simplicity. Adorning occasions worthy of remembering.

Fern, knitted together, lush green breath, growing out, covering. Plant or a tree.

Angel, your wings guard, they guide, your beautiful expand protects. You cover me Angel wings.

Calla, Soft and secure, unfolds gently bestowing beauty.

Iris, Soft petals folding into each other, expressions of humility.

Hyacinth, vibrant budding bundles breaking in the direction of love.

Holly, droplets, twinkles on a branch, break invisible barriers to bring nature to life.

Buttercup, winding rings that curve and cascade.

Azalea, a plethora of colors springing up in dry places, ushering life and eastern light.

Camellia, planted in glossy green gardens, evergreen basket holding beautiful petals.

Blossom, holding onto the strength inside, woven tightly together until bloom.

Forget Me Not, if you do, I won't mind. For there is room for new memories.

Lilac, you are who you are. Indigo. You sprung up in the garden as the seasons alarm. Spring is here. Eastern homeland, now you've flown west.

Marigold, folds of French, African, and Mexican gold bursting into every direction. A striking, yet patient blossoming floret.

Tansy, gather the joy that is within, share it with world, you shine like the sun.

Rosemary, hearty, steady, distinguished.

Bell, knocking, knocking until opportunity opens, your bloom is beauty to behold.

Heather, hope springs from you. It drips off your edges, like fresh water off a mountaintop that flows into the sea.

Pink, blended refrains of red and white, unafraid of what other say you are.

You are Pink.

Viola, I never knew. I thought you only came in one color, but you are Viola. Violet, purples, indigo, yellows, oranges, white and so much more. You are so much more.

Ginger, growing higher in the arms of a powerful air, lifted to the sky.

Salvia, sultry clusters, cover the earth with red.

Sweet Pea, you are delicate. Your fresh refined aroma reaches our memories and reminds us that sweet is possible.

Veronica, vibrant purple, pink, and blues blossom grow towards the sun. You move in a cluster of change, blossoms petite and powerful. You are a bold brilliant color.

Armor of God

I will wear your name across my chest.
Because you alone are my righteousness.
I will honor you and wear your righteousness daily.
God you are my protection and you are my breastplate of righteousness.

I will hold your words to everything that comes my way.
Everything that tries to stop me, or put me in bondage, or try to take my life.
You are my sword. You are my strength, and you are the living word.
I will carry your writings in my heart and in my hand as my sword.

You are my belt that holds me up right, so that I will stand.
You pull me together when I feel weak, and I'm wrapped me up in your truth.
You told me that you'd never leave, and you have never left my side.
You are fastened to my waist, pulling me closer to you, you hold me, I belong to you.

Where my feet land I pray is where your word sends me.
I want to share the word you have lived and written. The news of the risen Savior.
Remind me of a sweet aroma that glides through the air, and lands in front of you.
It's an honor to share you, telling your good news.

These words are walking, and these are walking shoes.
These words are for talking, and these words they are talking to you.

It gets heavy to carry at times, but I know that it will save my life.
This shield that protects my body is keeping the danger out.
The faith I need to protect me, is the faith that is hard to bear.
I know I must fully depend on you, and that you will protect me.

I fear no one, I only fear you, and so I desire to honor, to respect you.
I will hold onto you like a tree holds onto its roots — faithfully.
This shield was made to protect me, behind this shield is where I hide.
Your love is my shield.

Inside my mind is your plan for my life.
Your helmet of salvation protects it.
From the attacks of the enemy,
From the challenges and losses in life.

My helmet, your salvation, this mind, is in Christ.
Renewed in Yeshua, growing in the Immanuel's love.
Under the protection of your blood, your blood works.
The living water washes my mind daily. Transformation through purification.

I said Lord, God, save me, and you said, "It is done."
Your unfailing love is my helmet.
Your faithfulness, your enduring love, forever present, your love is above all.
You are my helmet, you are my Salvation.

You are my God, you are my Daddy,
My Heaven Father, my everything.
You are my armor,
My Amor of God.

Pace Girl

Part Two

I see you walking fast.
Some say, "too fast."
Moving through the intersections of life.
Not disrupting anything in her path.
Only wanting to arrive.

She sees oncoming traffic.
She also sees her path.
She's walking with intention.
Don't try to stop her. She's on a mission.

When the winds of life whirl past her,
She shields her body from its harsh touch.
She is prepared for the weather of her everchanging life.
She has strong women in her corner. She is a strong woman.
She is walking in pace with her life.

She sees oncoming traffic.
She also sees her path.
She's walking with intention.
Don't try to stop her. She's on a mission.

She can see the goal it's in her view.
She knows that it's around the bend.
She stops only to rest and refuel.
She knows that she has an opponent who wants to stop her,
But that won't change her pace, not this girl.

She sees oncoming traffic.
She also sees her path.
She's walking with intention.
Don't try to stop her. She's on a mission.

She arrives.
She has made it.
But this isn't the end for her.
She wants so much more.
There's more work to be done, on the steady road to greatness—Pace Girl.

Lovely buds of May

Deemed the most beautiful.
Blooming blossoming buds from the Garden of Eden.
She is from the Mother of the Earth.
Her Ancestors are Kings.
Grandmother was a Queen.

And she is a maturing ripe fruit in the garden.
In time she will be ready to fall from the arms of the garden and onto the earth.
Until then she is a blossom blooming in May,
Waiting for the beautiful birth of her full brilliance on a summer day.

Poetry

Part two

Poetry, I remember that first "Buzz" about alliteration.
The prepositional phrase that first placed me under your whimsical ways.
The first simile that made me smile.
The personification of your long reaching arms.
Poetry you take to me to new heights.
To depths that my feet could never reach.

You alone are my metaphorical blanket of warmth.
Covering me with your everything, you secure me in your words. Your words, your word.

Poetry your words have changed me.
Your words have raised me.
I remember the infant me.
Barely able to form an end rhyme.
Crawling across blank paper,
hoping to finish in rhythmic time.

Fumbling through a forest of scribbled words, eraser marks,
and after thoughts.

Yes, you Poetry have nurtured me through it all.
You watched me learn how to walk.
Until I stood without a wobble.
Until I walked across the length of each 8 by 11.
Until I stood firm in what you taught me.
I walked into who I was meant to be—In you Poetry.

Poetry in you, poetry in you I am,
poetry in you I can be.

Poetry you have held me up when I was weak.
Poetry you have been my words when I could not speak.
Poetry you have been my song.
When I could not bellow out sounds of pain or joy from me diaphragm.
Poetry you have been the braze to my once twisted my mind.
Poetry you are the ligaments holding the limbs of my imagination together.

You have been the bandage to my wounded piercing pain, to my beaten and bruised eyes.
I survived only to fall into the safety of your arms.

Poetry you are my medic your holistic drinks changes my inside and my outside.
You've shown me that I didn't need artificial love to be healed—only you.
You gave me space to formulate the words.
The words that would one day set me free.
Your patient pause—has room enough for all my broken battered needs.
Poetry you've showed me that you could wait for me.

Poetry, you allowed me to move through the atmosphere of lines.
Poetry you taught me to navigate through the rows and stanzas of my mixed emotions.

Poetry you help me find joy, love, and peace.
I laid my heart out for the world to see, but I wasn't alone you graced the mic with me.
Each time I rhymed, you chimed, each time you chimed, I rhymed.
Poetry you've partied with me too—remember that time we did that freestyle.
As hot as like a summer day.
The stage was our plate and our rhymes made the perfect dish.

Poetry you did that. Poetry you did that.
Poetry you did that.

Poetry you have been my mother, cradling me during stormy nights.
Declaring that nothing could stop me, and in you I would be safe.
That in your words I will be can do anything I imagine.
Poetry you are my father protecting me from harm.
Assuring me that nothing would prevail against me.
Poetry your love, your strength, can and will protect me forever.

Poetry your love. Poetry your love is.
Poetry your love is.

Poetry you are my sister.
Staying up with me all hours of the night listening to my stories.
Always letting me speak first.
Never seeking your own attention.
Yet always giving room for us to exist together.
Poetry you are perfect like that.

Poetry you are perfect.
Perfect Poetry, perfect Poetry.

Perfect poetry you are everything I need and so much more.
Poetry you are my brother.
Picking apart every person I've ever liked or dared to be with.
Wondering, what their motives are, and what are they looking for?
Poetry, you always want to know.
Why their eyes don't match yours—you're not looking for a quitter.

Poetry you look into the eyes of my life. Poetry you look into my eyes for life.
Poetry you look into the eyes of life.

Poetry you'll tell me what you think.
You'll tell the truth without one blink.
Poetry, you are never overbearing.
Yet you bare all.
Poetry you are silent at times,
but you never stay that way for long.

Poetry you are. Poetry you are.
Poetry you are.

You are my perfect poetry.
Now I can walk, run, and sprint through the thoughts in my mind.
Now I can decipher them all with your wisdom and your meticulous eye.
Now I can sail across an ocean of rhymes.
Knowing that I will not drown in the thoughts in my mind,
or in the next rhyme.

Having faith that all we've been through will be sufficient in getting me through the next stage of life—and it is.

Poetry,
Poetry you are there for me.
Poetry I want you to always be.
Poetry I love you too, because I know you love me.
You always show me new ways to love.
Poetry, you except me, for me. Poetry you show I am worthy.

More suitable for your word play.
For your personifying and mystic ways.

So now I hold you,
Hold you close to my chest,
Hold you like I gave birth to you.
Like I was the one that breathed life into you.
Yet knowing that your existence was the breath that gave me life.
I Needed another breath—you gave me new lungs.

Knowing that I could not do this without you.
Knowing that I could not reach these heights without the ladder that your words created.

You're concrete.
You're secure me.
You're sure.
You're strong,
You're pure.
Poetry, you are all this world of words ever needed.

It was you. It was you.
It was you.

Poetry.
It was you—poetry.
Poetry it was you.
Poetry you changed this world.
Poetry I have joy, because you are in my life.
Poetry you are the joy in my life.

Chapter 6 Breakdown

Chapter Six: Greater Than

In this chapter, I took the liberty in being extremely positive, hopeful, optimistic, open-minded, and vulnerable to new thoughts and ideas. I knew that I still had some emotions, thoughts, and behaviors, I needed to continue to work through. The goal of this chapter was to reach for Greater Than. Greater wholeness in my heart, greater mental health, physical health, and life transformation. This meant writing in a safe space of self-love, self-actualization, and self-discovery artistically. As I continued to write I noticed my story was getting good, and I became excited to see what else the universe had for me, as I continue to live and write. Cheers to chapter 6 and beyond.

Greater Than

This poem is written as a letter, and is meant to speak love, peace, and hope into my life. I think we all need to have a reminded that I we are wonderful, so I wrote this.

Jamaica

The only place I consider home to this day, this poem is an expression of my longing to be in Jamaica.

Daughter

I don't have a daughter, nor am I expecting a child while I write this. Using imagination, I think what if I did have a daughter? What would I want and need her to know and understand about who she is? What would I want and need her to know about my love for her?

LOVE

In this chapter my conversations about love become clearer. My new thoughts of love are from a place of peace, understanding and knowledge, rather than pain and confusion.

Guidance

This poem acknowledges that as I walk through this new chapter in my life, I can only do it with Holy Spirit guidance.

Who I am, And Who I'm not

This poem is a memo or note to self, and I wanted self to know who she is and isn't.

Flaws

What do we use to hide our flaws, maybe you drink socially, maybe you are a people pleaser? Maybe you smoke, maybe you hide behind your fashion, or use your pain to hurt others so you have a temporary moment of feeling good? Are we so afraid that if people knew the true version of you, they may not like it? In this poem I learn to love my flaws, use them as a starting place for growth and love.

Happy: Newly defined

I call this Happy: Newly defined, because I noticed in my life people would volunteer their version of my happy and try to convince me that's what I needed to do. I wasn't keen to the idea of someone else, discarding what I saw as happy, and wanting me to do the same. So, I thought I'll define it for myself, so I know.

Good

This poem is a song on repeat. It's calling the greatness out of me, echoing the sound of hope and change, and then says, "you were made for this."

Won't look back

This poem is about knowing I needed to move forward, I was terrified to move out of familiarity the past offered. With reservations I moved forward and asked myself to accept that I could have a good life, a new life.

Wrapped

A beautiful singer and vocal couch taught me a song, and it resonates with me to this day. The idea of being wrapped in the love of God, to be covered by Him and protected by Him. In this poem, I'm making electing to move forward with my Love Relationship with God.

I Rise

This poem is about perseverance, hope, and how a person can rise above anything that tries to keep then down. I rise for my dreams, I rise in hopes to positively impact the people all over the world, and I rise for my family.

Spring Time

I love spring, and this poem depicts a few of my favorite parts of Spring.

Don't Want to Fall in Love

When I wrote this poem, I did not want to fall in love, I was tired of relationship heartaches and disappointments. Still I love to love. This poem speaks to a future me, and a future love that I know I needed. I knew the type of love this poem eluded to would be a true depiction of love. As I wrote the poem I thought 'Am I ready?'

Organic

This poem was written as conversation to my future love interest, I wrote to speak into the future I wanted.

Dear Me

A love letter to self, that allows a moment for honesty, openness and love to permeate into the heart.

Colors

At times in our life we need to see ourselves in a different light, and then consider living life in new version of you. A poem which calls for a new perspective and interpretation of self.

Girls, Women
This poem is about loving yourself where you're at, and being content with life at the stage you're in.

Morning
This poem was about being present and welcoming to each day.

The Light
I wrote this poem to remind myself to be who I was called to be, and to not be afraid of who that person is and who she is growing and glowing into.

Fruits
Galatians 5:22-23 in the New Testament section of the Bible speaks about a way of being, and it's challenging. I wrote this poem as a way for me to find understanding and application of the words I read.

Wisdom
This poem is about seeing life in the best light, and to do that we need wisdom.

Flowers
I love flowers, and I thought how awesome it would be to write a poem about the beautiful strength that make women who they are, through the lens of flowers.

Armor of God
This is my expression of a great prayer scripture found in Ephesian 6: 10-18; which suggests that each person show have a special type of armor on daily.

Pace Girl: Part Two
The follow up to "Pace Girl: Part One," I thought this poem needed two parts. I had to, and I wanted there to be a distinct change in her pace, her mindset, and her movement in this second poem. She has grown, she is growing, Pace Girls, you have grown, and you are growing.

Lovely buds of May
A poem about the right season for something blossom, and it can be any month as long as the timing is right.

Poetry: Part Two
This poem is about poetry and everything I've been through with poetry right by my side. There's so much said in this poem you can interpret this one.

Afterward

I used to think this book was about pain, and misfortune, how horrible life was for me. And horrible life must be for children that live in "guardian style environment without their biological parents." I used to think that I only wrote things about how much pain, I felt during horrible times of my life. I thought while writing this book, "woman your life was the worst, like how did you even survive or live through all that?" I'm amazed often that I have lived beyond the years of abuse. Amazed that I have a master's degree, with aspiration to have a PhD, and another Masters. Now to be an author, this is mind-blowing. I know this only the beginning of the good life I began to write about towards the end of the book.

I am so blessed to in the "land of the living" like the Bible says. Pain has nothing on the Joy that I have in my heart, and regret has nothing on the Love I now experience daily. Life is good when you take out the trash. Take out the trash thoughts that say, you will not live a happy life, that you've gone through too much, sinned too much (Christ already died for that, don't let your sin keep you stuck in a life you're not happy with). You are not forgotten, there are people who care about you. Consider the idea that *love* is *greater than* all of life's horrific situations, that make a person never want to love again. Take out the trash, and try to stop listening to the lies that run carelessly in your mind and in your life, and watch your life change.

In the Bible John chapter 14:12, it says, "… Truly I say to you, he that believes in me, the works that I do, He will do even greater things than these, because I am going to the Father."

The supernatural movements in my life helped me to realize just how much love is copiously *Greater Than* all the painful moments in my life. Now I look at **Greater Than: Life's Journey Through Poetry** as a reminder of Jesus's promise to us in *John 14:12*. In the verse 12 above, Jesus is telling us to do greater than the works that he did. Not due to us being greater than Him, because he will endow us with the power to do greater. This was such an encouraging word during writing process. At first, I couldn't see the light at the end of the tunnel, everything was pitch black. I was still living in fear, but I wrote my way out of depression and wrote myself very own Greater Than. What I loved is while I wrote, I realized with each poem God gave to write, he also gave for my healing.

For you the reader, look at all the wonderful things you've done. I may not know you or haven't met you, but I believe God, who says that you are *"very good" Genesis 1:31*. With that said, I am going to assume you have done good things for yourself in your life and the lives of others, and that is not a small thing. Isn't it interesting how the good we do, is sometimes dwarfed by the bad we've done in the past? Don't let your good deeds go overlooked by YOU. Stay the path as narrow as it may be, and stay the course as hard as it may get. I entreat in life love more than you hate, laugh more than you cry, feel more than you don't, and choose to have joy and peace more than regret and worry. Of all the things I've learned thus far, these are the most powerful.

It is such a joy, and an amazing blessing to have been able to share this part of me with you, the reader. Against my reservations, I decided to be extremely transparent in this book. This level of openness is a mission to take on, in of itself. I truthfully never thought I would share my story as openly as I did with you here. Now, the same life I thought I couldn't live through, has become **Greater Than** life. Suddenly I moved from surviving, to living, and from living to wanting to live, and from wanting to live to growing up in **LOVE**.

I hope that while reading, you have become open to new ideas of what love truly is. Let new ideas of love grow in your heart and mind. I must admit the Lord has shown me unequivocally that *"... all things work together for good..." for those who love God, for those who are called according to His purpose... **Romans 8:28***. I couldn't have imagined this book was the beginning of my all things working together. I didn't think people like me could have good lives, let alone successful ones. I am blessed to see the other side of my life open-up like the clouds parting after a stormy day. I hope you enjoyed reading about my journey from fear to Freedom. I hope you find a *Greater Than* hope in your days. Thank you for reading this journey from broken to healed. It has been great talking to you all, here's to life after Chapter 6. I hope you live your "Greater Than" story daily.

About the Author

Halima A. Brown

I was born in beautiful island of Jamaica. For most of my life, I've resided on the eastern coast of United States. In a family of 10 children, I am 1 of 5 girls. It's a large family composed of siblings in multiple countries, but distance doesn't make heart love anyone of them less. Some random facts about me are, I like many enjoy travelling, all things outdoors, fitness, and I am a foodie to my core. Being a native of Jamaica I love the aquatic: swimming in the sea, diving into waterfalls, canoeing on rivers or lake, jet-skiing. Some of my hobbies are reading, roller-skating, watching movies, knitting, and getting lost for fun. Born a happy person, I love to dance, laugh and smile, and I love people. I am is beyond herself to be able to begin to present my writings with you.

Currently I live in Los Angeles, California. I am also Dancer, Teacher, and a Visual Artist. I attend several worship services weekly, host a woman only bible study, and women only open mic. And now I am starting to see myself in ministry now more than ever. I am is actively pursuing a love relationship with YHWH; which is colossal considering my past relationship ups and downs with GOD.

I am is also an educator and social worker. Receiving a Social Work degree in Buffalo, NY, then later received a Master's in Higher Education online. My goal is to continue my education, but for now I'm focused on living in my Artistic self. I've decided the nerd in me needs a break. The goal of my art is to use my life experiences and my imagination, as I write fictional characters in future works, is to cultivate healing for all women. As a writer I have a blast exploring life's nuances creatively. Through my Visual Artist I create paintings of vibrant, strong colorful women my desire is to capture portrayals of the female voice and female community. It is a balancing act at times being an Artist and an Educator, but I am confident in God, that I will be able to do both successfully.

One of my ultimate passions and what I see as my mission, is working with women and children. This desire and mission to help women is now a major driving forces for my writings. Art has healing powers. There's a possibility that self-expression can help females (all my readers) contemplate, work-through, examine their emotions, mental health and spiritual well-being to heal, let go, and grow. I hope my art, my writings will be a source of encouragement and inspiration to you women, and men in their journey to healing, health and a happy life. There's so much more I want to share, so check out the next page.

What's Next?

Upcoming Projects

- Children's Book: Highlighting the love and admiration a child has for her parents. A Second Children's Book, about a bright, brilliant, beautiful baby girl, who has taken over her Mom's life for the good. This story depicts how a child's love can bring the very best out of us.

- A Novel: A smart and witty novel. You'll enjoy this story as you follow the characters who think they can do it all alone, until they see two is better than one.

- Poetry: You can expect more poetry, this time about nature, music, travel, love, and so much more.

- Faith-based and encouraging books about life.

- Art: Halima, is working on a series of paintings based on Women, that will be showcased in Los Angeles, California.

Contact Halima A. Brown

Have questions and want to discuss the book? Do you have event or speaking engagement you'd like to book her for? Maybe you just want to pick her brain on how I did it? Or you want to talk about something you're are going through, she'd love to hear from you.

Booking E-mail: ArtistHalima@Gmail.com
Author E-mail: HalimaABrown@AuthorHalima.com
Instagram: WORDSWALK or WOMEN ONLY OPEN MIC

*Always remember that **LOVE** is **GREATER THAN** everything.*